Note from MAST Publishing House

Shannon Thomas, LCSW is the best-selling author of *Healing from Hidden Abuse: A Journey Through the Stages of Recovery from Psychological Abuse*, and the owner/lead therapist of an award-winning counseling practice in Southlake, TX. After dropping out of high school yet persevering to eventually earn her master's degree at age 34, to losing her father to a violent crime and her mother to addiction and mental illness, Thomas understands the need to overcome. As a leading therapist and survivor, Thomas is one of the few in the field to bridge the gap between pop culture and clinical advice.

Thomas has been featured in top media outlets including Business Insider, Teen Vogue, Elite Daily, Bustle, and Romper. Her first book, *Healing from Hidden Abuse*, is an international bestseller, has been published in multiple languages, and serves as a roadmap for book studies and host groups in ten countries and 43 states across the United States. Thomas also coined the "Six Stages of Healing" model, which has been met with favorable reviews and high applause from readers and medical professionals across the world. As part of her continued commitment to impact the masses and provide healing, Thomas shares ongoing perspectives through the lens of a therapist and fellow survivor of psychological abuse on her blog (shannonthomas.com/blog).

SHANNON THOMAS, LCSW

Best-Selling Author of Healing from Hidden Abuse

EXPOSING FINANCIAL ABUSE

WHEN MONEY IS A WEAPON

MAST Publishing House

Exposing Financial Abuse: When Money is a Weapon

Editor: Jenay Fritz
Cover Design and Layout Design: Ty Richards

ISBN: 978-0-9978290-2-0

DISCLAIMER

The content in this book is for educational and informational purposes only, and not for the purpose of providing individualized mental health advice. Your purchase, downloading and/or reading of these materials does not create a therapist-client relationship between Exposing Financial Abuse, the author, and you. The author and publisher make no representations or warranties about the completeness of the information, and expressly disclaim any implied warranties or merchantability or fitness for a particular purpose. If you have questions concerning your emotional or mental health, or about the application of the information described in this book, consult a qualified healthcare professional.

Dedicated to those who are healing from hidden abuse.
You are an inspiration.
Thank you for allowing me to journey along with you.

#healingfromhiddenabuse

CONTENTS

INTRODUCTION   1

1 LIES   15

2 THREATS   55

3 BASIC NEEDS   75

4 CRIMES   105

5 SABOTAGED   125

6 TURNING POINT   151

7 PROTECTION   177

8 REBUILDING   207

INTRODUCTION

Financial abuse. Not a light or easy topic. That's perfectly okay with me. I prefer real and raw, rather than watered down or maintaining a state of denial. The time has come for the reality of financial abuse to be exposed.

Apart from individuals who have been abused financially, most people have no idea what the terms financial abuse or financial exploitation really mean. Within the following pages, I'll pull back the cloak that covers this form of significant harm and expose it for all to see. Abusers bank on their behaviors being left in the dark and isolated. Since little is known or written on the topic of relational financial abuse, perpetrators are able to go unchallenged with their calloused and life-altering behaviors.

Test yourself. Right now, how would you describe financial abuse and exploitation? Perhaps you would say that it happens when someone's identity is stolen by a stranger who obtained their private information. Or, you may say something about elder abuse and how senior citizens are targeted by unscrupulous scam artists.

Those two descriptions are correct but are only the tip of the iceberg of what we're going to uncover together. Would you have thought financial abuse is perpetrated by a mom, dad, sibling, boyfriend, girlfriend, friend, religious leader, or most frequently, a spouse? Financial abuse and exploitation is quietly happening all around us, hidden within our neighborhoods and communities. You probably know someone on a personal level who lives in a financially abusive household and have absolutely no idea.

Could you tell who's controlled by money while volunteering at your kid's school? Would you be able to point out the person who carries the full burden of keeping the secret that money is a weapon within their life? I assure you, financial abuse doesn't come wrapped up in the package you'd expect, which is exactly my motivation for writing this book. We all need to have the collective understanding of how money is being used to entrap, control, and abuse the people around us. Hidden financial abuse.

In my first book, *Healing from Hidden Abuse: A Journey Through the Stages of Recovery from Psychological Abuse*, I introduced the Six Stages of Healing from psychological abuse. I developed these stages of recovery while working as a trauma therapist and through research conducted prior to writing the book. *Healing from Hidden Abuse* walks the reader through the stages of Despair, Education, Awakening, Boundaries, Restoration, and Maintenance. It covers psychological abuse in families, romantic relationships, friendships, the workplace, and religious communities. Hidden abuse is happening all around us but because of its covert nature, can be difficult to recognize and even harder to describe.

This new project, *Exposing Financial Abuse: When Money is a Weapon*, is the second book in the *Healing from Hidden Abuse* series. Why did I choose financial abuse to write about next? If survivors are shamed into not talking about psychological abuse in general, economic exploitation comes with an extra layer of intense humiliation.

Money being used as a weapon occurs across all demographics and financial income brackets. Women and men are both targets of financial harm. This form of abuse knows no boundaries and is caused by abusers who are either passively or overtly controlling all of the financial resources. It also happens when toxic individuals limit access to bank accounts or refuse to contribute equally and place a heavy burden on the other individual in the relationship. Sabotage plays a large role in the effectiveness of financial abuse.

Within the pages of *Exposing Financial Abuse: When Money is a Weapon*, you'll be given the opportunity to pull back the curtain and see into the lives of those who have

4

been financially harmed by someone close to them. Being able to take a closer look at this hidden world is a unique gift that cannot be taken lightly or without honor for those who have chosen to allow us into the most personal aspects of their lives.

If you're a survivor of financial abuse, I'm incredibly sorry that you have been touched by this form of malicious behavior. I hope within the pages of this book you'll find comfort in knowing you're absolutely not alone and will now have a resource to share with others to explain what you've lived through as a victim. I also hope you're able to slowly climb out of the vast hole this form of abuse leaves behind.

Recovery from financial abuse can be overwhelming and often feels hopeless. Its destruction and daily impact on the lives of its victims lasts much longer than even the toxic relationship. Many survivors have shared with me that years after the abuse ended, the financial damage remained. Financial restoration is one of the injuries on the psychological abuse spectrum that takes the longest to heal.

In preparation for this book, I conducted a qualitative research project. If you're not familiar with research, it basically means I asked several questions about financial abuse and people anonymously responded in their own words. Their stories are the heart and soul of *Exposing Financial Abuse: When Money is a Weapon*. Without their brave participation, we may never know the reality of financial abuse and exploitation. This type of harm hides in plain sight on the streets of our neighborhoods, on the sidelines of the soccer field as we cheer our kids on, within meetings at work, sitting in the same row at our religious place of worship, and at the table next to you at a restaurant.

Before we go any further, I want to thank all of the participants of the study whose stories we get to read within these pages. If you participated and you don't find your personal experience within the book, please know that I still read each one that was submitted. They all played a defining role in the tone and structure of this book. I couldn't have done this without your participation and am truly grateful for you. You gave not only your time, but your words were filled with honesty, heartbreak, seething anger, overwhelming fear, yet hope that life could someday become financially stable.

What exactly is financial abuse?

The answer to these questions can serve as a starting point to understanding this form of harm.

- Has your partner ever moved money from your joint account to their individual account without your prior knowledge or consent?

- Did your ex-spouse hide his or her income from being included in the calculations for child and/or spousal support?

- Has someone close to you forged your name on a financial document?

- Does your ex-spouse suddenly stop paying child support as a means of furthering their abuse and control over your life?

- Has your spouse or parent taken out lines of credit in your name without your consent?

- Does your spouse or ex-spouse use his/her business or commission-based employment as a means of hiding their true income?

- Are you blamed for creating financial stress, but are not the one who overspends?

- Have your religious leaders said that you must give to the church first, even if that means you cannot provide for your household's basic needs?

- Have you found secret checking, savings accounts, or investment accounts opened by your spouse or partner as the sole owner?

- Is the family court system used by your estranged spouse or ex-spouse as a means of draining your financial resources?

- Have you gone without needs or wants but your spouse or partner freely spends joint money on themselves?

- Do you carry the full burden of making enough money for your household because your partner refuses to maintain steady employment?

- Do your parents use financial gifts as an open door to demand future compliance on your part?

What does financial abuse look like in daily life? Here's a quick preview of the type of real life stories we're going to cover within the pages of *Exposing Financial Abuse*:

> *I slept on a mattress on the floor my entire pregnancy because he said we couldn't afford a bed. We had no water in our home the first winter because he said we couldn't afford it. He would be gone 90% of the time so it was me and my children living in this environment. He made over $8k a month but the money went to his affairs. I was given $300 a month for food and necessities as my allowance to provide for me and my two teens."*

– Gem

"

He would withhold money (my allotment) unless I would give him what he wanted sexually. He would say things like, 'Why should I be a husband to you if you're not being a wife to me.'"

– Ashley

"

My ex-wife told me that choosing to buy groceries for our family would bring God's wrath upon our household. I was continually told that we would never be blessed if we did not give above and beyond our 10% tithe. I was told I had a "compulsive overspending" [problem] anytime I purchased anything she did not personally think I or the children needed, or if it wasn't something God told her we could have."

– Rob

"*On the very day I filed for divorce he was unexpectedly "fired" from his job as COO of a large manufacturer. He did not collect any unemployment and was able to convince the court that he could only pay the minimum of $500/mo in child support. Child was 4 at the time and is now 16. He has not worked since at a job that is documented for taxes. In the same time frame he has purchased a new Audi, a yacht, and a waterfront condo.*"

– Chris

"*My parents were very wealthy but every piece of clothing I bought was inspected (including my bras) by my step-mother to determine whether I could keep them or not. It became so uncomfortable and created such anxiety for me, I began buying clothes from the lost and found at school and old clothes from my friends.*"

– Zia

11

> *I was lucky... I had the financial resources and a very good job to keep everything going for our family. However, I had responsibly saved and planned for retirement from the time I was 23 years old and most of that is now gone and I am having to start over at 47."*

– Susan

> *He worked at a church and there was no accountability to the congregation of his spending and would spend thousands of dollars for a new laptop when he didn't need one. That was just the things we knew. The way he spent and used the church credit card and had access to funds with his lack of wisdom and sense of entitlement and no concern for the fact this was God's tithe from the congregation was looking very concerning."*

– Stacy

I continue to work at the business that I built, and he did everything he could to destroy. I am a real estate broker owner. At 76. I get up every day and go to work."

- PJ

These are real people. They're telling you about things that actually took place in their lives. These aren't compilations of different stories. The research project had over 450 individual participants. The majority were women, but I know that men have been targets of financial abuse just as much as their female counterparts. Want to know what surprised me the most about the people who responded? A whopping 63 percent said they were in a financially abusive relationship within the last three years to present day. For 63 percent, financial abuse is a current crisis happening in their lives. The fact that financial abusers and exploiters are negatively impacting so many lives is scandalous.

1

LIES

Oh, the lies financial abusers tell. They tell small lies. They tell big lies. They tell huge damaging lies. It's as if the truth is something they create, shift, and mold for their own whims. There are no absolute truths in the world of an economic abuser. No universal moral compass that guides their actions. Truth is what they create in their mind and then they act accordingly.

I sat there reading through the survivor stories shaking my head in utter disbelief. The audacity of abusers never ceases to disgust me, and I've witnessed this phenomenon through my work as a trauma therapist. You would think at some point I'd stop being shocked by the level that some people are willing to sink to. The depths and reality of financial harm even stunned me, and I thought I'd heard and seen it all.

Why do we start with exposing the lies that financial abusers tell? Lies are the foundation of this form of harm. They set the stage for the financial abuse to play out and progress into deeper levels of damage.

> *My husband told me that we were on the brink of poverty, when in fact he had over $200,000 in the bank, two houses (one of which was paid off), over $750,000 in 401k and retirement accounts and received a monthly income from rental off the paid-off house. None of which I had access to even though we were together for 30 years."*

- CC

There are several key elements of financial abuse within CC's story. Notice that they were together over three decades, but she wrote "he had over $200,000 in the bank." In their world, it was his money. CC came to believe the money, houses, and the retirement accounts were his alone because of the lies he told. The falsehoods were probably repeated to her over and over again until they became the truth in both words and actions. The money was his and he didn't need to share it with her.

There's no way a couple can be together for over thirty years and have one person claim it's only his or her money. Thirty years as a couple includes the early building blocks of financial wealth and stability, the melding of two lives together for a very long time. Three decades deserves acknowledging the partnership of the couple but instead, some fall into very traditional patriarchal roles where the husband handles the finances with little input or involvement from the wife. In these situations, we often see limited or no access to the family wealth. The wife is held to whatever allowance or credit limit the husband establishes and nothing more. Many spouses don't even know the full picture of their family financial portfolio or how to log into bank accounts. They only know what they're told, which is a perfect environment for damaging lies to take root and flourish.

> *He relentlessly pressured me into buying stocks with money I inherited. Within a week they were worthless and then demanded to take the write-off for his personal taxes after the divorce. He lied that the share of medical practice spin-off was worthless and*

*after the divorce it was worth 4 million.
He bought an empty lot behind our
house to build a place for his mother
(who was remarried) but he confessed
after [the] divorce it was to build on
it for his new wife and live behind me
and the kids to keep an eye on us.
He told the judge he had no income but
admitted he had not submitted billing
for 6 months- the magic # for child
support calculations."*

- Mave

Pressuring a spouse to use their inheritance to buy stocks that suddenly became worthless doesn't sound like a coincidence but a calculated lie. How does this work as a benefit for a financial abuser? Perhaps the inheritance wasn't going to be used in a manner that pleased the spouse, so he orchestrated to have the money wasted in a back-door way for a personal financial tax benefit. Relentless pressure is a tool used by those who financially exploit other people. They keep pushing until they get their way and use multiple angles that all come back to their own gain.

> *He said for years he couldn't afford to pay me my allowance. (Withholding truth) He had me work for free caring for my handicapped brother overnight for 6 months, to pay off the "rent" he was charging me while I went to college. I found out later that the state had paid my parents money to pay the caregiver, so I should have received those funds and then [paid] him rent (although I don't think he should have charged me rent in the first place)."*

– Tamra

Taking advantage of family members is sadly common in dysfunctional households. The get-what-you-can mentality and using one another is a daily occurrence. Tamra was available to care for her brother and her dad lied by withholding the truth that he was receiving payment for her caregiving. Where did that money go? Into her dad's pockets, while Tamra worked overnight to care for her brother and pay off a "debt" of rent in her own family's home.

20

What is at the root of a parent taking advantage of their own child? A lack of attachment at a core level. When people don't properly bond to their caregivers in their own childhood and adolescence, they go on to become toxic parents. Financial abuse perpetrated by parents always involves a level of tragic disconnect with their children. We cannot use people we truly care about.

> *I worked 2 full-time (40+ hours each) jobs and was still the primary caregiver for our child-she would not work but continually ran up large debt on QVC or Jewelry TV. I was struggling to keep utilities turned on and she would buy $1,300 rings that she had nowhere to even wear."*
>
> **- Mitchell**

Financial abuse happens not only through control and dominance of resources, but by spending money in a way that keeps the budget tight and the target of the abuse working harder to keep up with the spending. The perfect set up happens when someone spends as much or more than what the household earns while the victim is too busy trying to stay afloat financially to find a way out of the trap. Mitchell was busy parenting their child, working 80 hours a week, and trying to keep the utilities on. However, his spouse was spending money on items that brought no value to their family. Selfishness is at the heart of economic exploitation.

> *Because he withheld all financial information from me, I would go to the grocery store and have my checks declined. Multiple times, I had to leave an entire cart at the register, because our account was overdrawn (and I didn't know it)."*
>
> **- Joy**

Embarrassment. Abusers don't care if they create situations where their family is publicly humiliated. Joy's partner kept vital financial information from her and it led to standing at the cash register embarrassed because they didn't have enough money to buy groceries. Not only is the moment tragic because she didn't know where they stood financially, but she had to leave her food behind.

Did Joy's financial abuser think about the moments that were created by keeping her out of the loop regarding their finances? Probably not. He was most likely too busy thinking about his own needs to think about her walking out of the grocery store empty-handed.

> *I had to live with the knowledge of his intention to divorce in secret and in silence for seven months because he was a pastor and did not want to jeopardize that work. During that time, he denied me access to our mutual bank account. [This] continued for months after he moved out of our home. And I had to begin to request a free lunch for my three children, and other forms of assistance all the while living in a very large home in a very nice neighborhood."*

– Pammie

23

Living in an affluent neighborhood and being a pastor's wife is not a buffer from being financially exploited. When a spouse is in a high-profile position, the lies are more deeply buried behind the shiny image that has been artificially created. Pammie's financially abusive pastor husband chose to cut off their bank account funds. You may be wondering how this is possible. I can tell you that in many jurisdictions, until formal paperwork is filed with the courts, spouses have the power to move money as they choose. If a spouse decides to clear out the mutual bank account, they can and often do when one spouse is toxic. The victim spouse will have to use the court system to gain access to their funds. In the meantime, kids need food for lunch. Pammie did what she had to do, and that was provide for her three kids even without access to her own money.

> *Lies about her planned retirement so that we could focus on her career for a period of time and then mine once she retired. I put my life and interest on hold, managed her career, ran our company, and she never intended*

on retiring during the agreed timeframes. When we broke up, I was all but starting my life over and she carried on with her career still to this day. She was supposedly going to retire in 2011."

- Olivia

Financial deception comes in the form of taking advantage of other people, with little to no regard for the victim's well-being. People become objects that are used for what they can gain. In Olivia's situation, her time, energy, and skills were used to focus on the abuser's life, while putting her own hopes and goals on hold. She was willing to do this because it was supposed to be temporary. Healthy relationships often involve one person stepping up to support the other for a certain period of time and with clear goals in mind. However, one thing I've learned is that financial abusers will lie and create elaborate stories to hide their exploitive intentions and get as much out of their targets as they can. Olivia was used and then left to play catch up for the years she poured into her spouse's financial growth instead of her own.

25

The only thing I wanted for my wedding was a wonderful honeymoon, so we didn't ask for gifts or anything just if people wanted to do something for us they could contribute towards our honeymoon. My husband resisted any kinds of reservations or formal plans for as long as possible. Our honeymoon was going to be at some point at least a month or more after our wedding so that we knew how much we had to spend for it. We ended up having around $1,000, and in the end, we ended up going to a football game on Thanksgiving in San

Francisco and stayed at an in-laws relatives house while they were out of town. We drove over 7 hours each way and one of the only things I was asking for was to stay at a B&B for one night at some point on the trip, possibly on the way back. He kept telling me that we didn't have the money for it and that we should save the money that we had bills to pay. In the end, we didn't end up staying anywhere besides the relative's house and he ended up purchasing new computers for his own business that he had started six months prior."

– Nicole

In the world of abusers, your needs don't matter. Not even what you want for your own honeymoon. Many financial abusers exhibit behavior that closely mirrors narcissistic features. It's always about them and their needs, wants, plans, and goals. Nicole wanted one evening in a bed and breakfast for her honeymoon road-trip. That isn't asking a lot. At all. What Nicole wanted was within a normal range based on their budget. Her new husband didn't value staying in a nice hotel but more importantly, he didn't value Nicole's wish. He passive-aggressively dragged his feet until he got his way. He wanted to stay with relatives and use the wedding gift money to buy computers for his business. His wants, his needs, his goals, and his computers.

"*No, we don't lose money when I travel to China [for work]." (He has been paying prostitutes for sex our entire 25-year marriage and traveling to China for sex tourism under the guise of business trips). "I deserve to buy this to make up for all the time I 'have to' spend traveling."*

Admitting to having spent $1,600 on prostitutes, when it was tens of thousands of dollars over decades.

"It's not your money."
(I've been a stay at home mom.)

"I'm selling stock to pay for [the kids'] college." (He was taking out loans.)

"We don't have enough money to pay the mortgage."

"We can't afford that."

"I can't give you maintenance [anymore]. I don't have any money."

"I'm hemorrhaging money."

"I didn't spend too much."

"BMWs hold their value."

"You need to cut back on your spending."

"I'm really scared about our financial situation."

"I stay up at night thinking about money."

"You have to go back to work."

"You don't need to work."

"You're not good enough to be a professional."

"I will handle the bill paying, because you're not doing a good job."

"I don't have to give you any of my money."

"You bought it, but it wasn't your money."

"I have no money to give you."

"Stop saying that I got a bonus from work."

"I don't know why you won't trust me."

"You don't need a credit card."

- Lauri

What Lauri so perfectly provides for us is the exact script of a psychologically abusive person whose weapon of choice is money. This list gives us a glimpse into the chaotic pattern of messages that abusers hurl at their victims. Funneling money into the international sex trade, yet having the audacity to ask, "why don't you trust me?" The abuser was attempting to place the duty of creating trust on Lauri's lap. It wasn't her duty to create trust in an environment that her spouse had poisoned.

Go back and re-read the list again. Imagine this dialogue taking place within one conversation. The rapid fire of confusion is a brainwashing technique that emotional and psychological abusers utilize. They like to create a vortex and use words to spin people so the victim leaves the conversation with full responsibility of making things better and harmonious with the abuser.

> *I received an inheritance. Before the estate was settled he would incur debt while telling whomever it was that "we were coming into money." As if it were his own inheritance! He also never*

repaid any debts. My financial situation went downhill after being with him. He controlled the finances and would get angry if I suggested that I handle the checkbook, etc. We ended up filing bankruptcy, losing our home. We were/ are both college educated professionals. I can't believe I allowed it to happen."

- Cynthia

Financial exploiters insert themselves into the lives of their targets. Cynthia was receiving the gift of inheritance from being part of a family who managed their resources well enough to leave a financial blessing. Cynthia's partner attached himself like a leech to that gift. He paraded around the idea that he was the one receiving the family gift and moved forward with spending it before the money had even hit the bank account.

What would cause someone to think so highly of themselves that they're okay with spending someone else's money as their own? Entitlement. Cynthia's spouse clearly felt entitled to her inheritance. From her own wording, I'll jump to the conclusion that she didn't give him the impression that the money was his to equally spend. Life taught this financial abuser that what was actually someone else's was his by default. He was entitled to Cynthia's inheritance, even if she didn't offer. Entitlement runs deep in all economic abusers and is one of the foundational bricks for this form of exploitation. It is embedded within every story.

> *I was told that she would get a job and help me pay for the cosmetic surgery that she wanted and needed for her to gain more self-confidence. So, she got a breast augmentation and a tummy tuck. So now here we are almost a year after the discard and there's a lawyer contacting me saying that I'm being sued for the procedure. Somehow my name was the only one on the application for credit. So, I'm stuck paying for something that she used to attract other men. And still a little bit bitter about it."*

– Josh

34

Josh was exploited by a female financial abuser. He was used financially, and his abuser left the bill in Josh's name. Do we know that she intended to use her new, improved body to attract other men and leave Josh? No, we don't know that for sure, but Josh suspected that to be the case. However, we do know that she purposefully left the doctor bill for him. That choice was made before the surgery. How do we know this? She left only his name as the responsible party. That's a choice. Financial abusers know what they're doing. They believe their needs are most important, and use people close to them to get their wants covered. Josh's abuser knew she didn't put her own name on the credit account with the cosmetic surgeon. These mistakes don't happen by accident.

Let's pause here and say yes, female abusers do exist as often as their male counterparts. I know that male stories of exploitation and abuse are out there because historically, half of my counseling clients have been men who are survivors of all forms of abuse (psychological, emotional, physical, sexual, financial, and spiritual).

"We (the initial idea really was mine and I also gave it the initial financial boost) set up the tour guide business for my ex-husband in the city we both lived in at the time. "The weather" was mostly the main element in how he couldn't get any money made. I heard it all. It was too sunny or nor sunny enough, the sun was shining too bright or in the wrong angle...the wind was blowing too much, it was blowing up the street and was unpleasant, and then down the street and it put people off, then it was the gusts of wind or too much dust in it... The best one was the rain (I live in Scotland - you

don't come here for the weather).
The rain was too persistent, too cold,
too drizzly, too heavy, too much
or simply too wet. My ex would call
me from the street describing these
weather situations and how there
are no people on the street and how
he was wasting his time standing
here waiting there for it to happen,
only to hear the crowd of people
cheering in the background watching
one of the street performers' show.
My ex always had a million reasons
why things didn't work out. He would
find the problem for every solution."

– Lubi

Thank you, Lubi, for participating in this project. I was pleased when I came across your story. Why? Because it perfectly highlights how a passive-aggressive financial abuser behaves. They lie about stupid things. They make up ridiculous excuses about the wind in Scotland when they're often just lazy. As Lubi said, they have a problem for every solution.

There are a few key components when it comes to the passive-aggressive financial abuser. One of the first steps these people take is creating the illusion that they're looking for work, doing a good job, or some other fake billboard about their efforts to contribute financially. Lubi's ex got out of bed, went down to the tourist area, and called Lubi to complain about the wind. Why would he make the effort to look like he was trying to earn an income? Aspects of image control are important to financial abusers. They want to hide their true motives, so they do just enough to keep the façade up that they're contributing financially. This is a lie though. Lazy abusers have no interest in the hard work it requires to be a reliable financial source for a couple or family.

> Lie: *"I'm not looking at a house to buy"*
> *"No, I'm not buying a house"*
>
> *Truth: we were sitting outside the judge's chambers while our lawyers were working on our settlement. His lawyer was arguing that I had plenty of cash and his client needed to take it from me to buy his new house. His salary is double mine and he had zero debt and 1/2 million in savings. He took me to court several times and paid thousands in legal fees just to take my money. He won - he got 90k in cash from me."*
>
> **- Gin**

Economic abusers lie about their future plans and have acting skills that could win awards because it allows them to calculate and implement their selfish intentions with the element of surprise. The bait and switch game works perfectly in the context of financial abuse. No, I'm not buying a house and won't be asking for more money to buy it. The truth? Gin was court-ordered to give her ex $90,000 and we can assume it went to his new house.

> *He told me I am part owner in his company, but I have no ability to access the money as he is telling me I am free to leave. He brainwashed me into thinking getting a job was ridiculous because I should be helping him with his business. I tried to help with the business, but he would smoke pot while telling what to put on the invoices, so it was like working with a 5-year-old. He refused to write a list out of what services cost what, so I would have to be a mind reader to actually do my job."*

– Catherine

Free to leave but no access to money. Now that's a perfect set up. Where does a survivor of this form of abuse go without enough finances? A shelter? Maybe. But why should someone be forced to leave behind the comforts of their home and any financial portfolios that were cultivated during the marriage or relationship? Why should one partner be allowed to keep all the money and assets, while the victim must rebuild their entire financial situation?

The financial abuser in Catherine's life presented two options – help run his business and have him as a business partner who expects her to read his mind because he can't focus or leave without access to the shared money. Those two options are neither realistic or acceptable.

> *Taught by the founding pastor at a church we were members of for eight years that if we didn't tithe our first 10% of gross income than the other 90% would be cursed by God. Taught that we tithe to the church over paying the electricity bill or putting food on the table. Taught that we need to pay God back if we miss a tithe even during hard financial times."*
>
> **– Babette**

Paying God back. Honoring God by giving financially to your local church. Is it a percentage of your gross or your net? Are you compelled through fear of being cursed by God or disciplined by church leaders? There are many beliefs about what rules devotees must follow for any specific religious faith. Babette shares what happens when financial abuse is co-mingled with spiritual abuse.

Religious leaders have a duty to teach what they believe are truths within their faith. However, it crosses a dangerous line when congregation members are shamed into giving financially to their place of worship and in doing so, neglect their need for food, clothing, housing, transportation, medical care, and the needs of their family members.

Some church leaders will say they understand if people cannot tithe (or give) the full 10 percent and encourage individuals to start with a smaller percentage and work up to 10. That sounds compassionate and not financially abusive. Nevertheless, the issue that comes along is that congregation members feel tremendous pressure to reach the 10 percent threshold. What happens if the individual or family's budget cannot, and will not, sustain 10 percent and is being taught that unless it's exactly 10 percent, then the rest is cursed?

The subtle nature of religious financial abuse is damaging to its targets and very controversial. Religious leaders will immediately use their theological beliefs and interpretations to justify their position. Some will even say they see themselves as helping congregation members live better lives by stressing the need to give 10 percent. Yet, abusive behaviors are always justified by the abuser. That's a universal truth.

"

That he wouldn't be able to afford to visit his child if I cashed his child support checks. I didn't cash them, and the visits never happened. When I finally took him to court over this and other money he owed me, he told the judge that the most he could afford to pay me was $50 month. One month later, I received a check for the $5,000 he owed me. (Courtesy of his current victim, no doubt.) He told me he was so broke that he could barely afford to pay rent, so I offered to start paying our child's health insurance premiums "until he got back on his feet." Turns out he was courting his next victim, shacking up with her and planning a wedding."

– Jen

Don't cash my child support checks or I won't have money to come visit my child, but I can plan a wedding with my new target. What a collection of lies and fraud by a financial abuser. If seeing his child was more valuable to him, he would move heaven and earth to make it happen. Instead, he put the responsibility on Jen to enable his immaturity and selfish choices of spending his money on courting his next victim instead of providing the mandated health insurance and visiting.

The truth? This story illustrates how scheming financial abusers will push their responsibilities on the person who's willing to make the sacrifices for the best interest of the family. Jen stepped up. She didn't cash the checks that she was legally and morally entitled to for the needs of their child. She also took on the financial duty of paying for health insurance. Guess what happened? Dad still didn't show up for visits with his kiddo. Why? He was busy living his life in a way that served his immediate satisfaction and being a dad didn't make the cut. This is the tragic reality of parental financial abuse related to divorce. The basic needs of the children are secondary to the selfish desires of the toxic parent.

> *That his whole paycheck was going into our joint account. After he died I discovered it was not. A portion of every pay was going into an account with his sister as the beneficiary."*

- 3 strikes

Did his sister know she was the benefactor of this secret bank account? Most likely and I'll go so far as to say she probably played an active part in creating the triangulation between this couple. Toxic in-law relationships are common and financial deception plays a key role in the unhealthy environment. In the world of psychological abuse, the people who support toxic individuals are known as "flying monkeys." This is a reference to the monkeys who worked for the witch in the movie, *The Wizard of Oz*. Apath is another term that can be used to describe these co-abusers.

An apath is the accomplice to an abuser. They function to normalize abnormal behavior. A sister who supports and helps hide funds as a means of financial abuse is a toxic collaborator. Her agreement was an act of encouragement to the abuser. How would things be different if this financial abuser was told heck no about participating in hiding funds

45

from his spouse? Abusers continue their behaviors because flying-monkeys and apaths create an environment where the abuse is no longer repulsive, but now encouraged by their active support.

> *When we first met he was an attorney who was making close to $250k a year (according to him). Shortly after we met, he closed down his practice to go and get his PhD. I found out during discovery of our divorce that he was actually disbarred."*
>
> **- Eliza**

Secret lives. Being disbarred and your partner not knowing is living in a flood of daily lies. Making a huge career change within a marriage must include both spouses mutually agreeing that it's in the best interest of the relationship. Unilateral life decisions made by one partner are dangerous and a red flag of abuse. Eliza met someone who had an income potential that could give her the quality of life she may have wanted for her future. Do spouses sometimes make career shifts and need their partner's support? Of course. What Eliza wasn't given was the ability to know the truth about the change in her family's income. Her husband lied about being disbarred and made up an excuse about wanting to get his PhD. Why is this considered financially abusive? Eliza's spouse changed the agreement regarding their income and lied about it. He hid the fact that he had failed so greatly at being an attorney that he was kicked out of the profession. Withholding that information from Eliza is abusive within the context of marriage.

'The bills are all paid.

The tag was taken because of a mistake made by the DMV not me.

The house isn't in foreclosure that's a mistake made by the bank.

I paid your car payment I don't know why they are repossessing it.

I borrowed that money, but we don't have to pay it back.

I'm buying lottery tickets only with the money I win back on them not household money.

I will add your name to the bank account soon.

I paid the IRS in payments the amount owed is paid now.

I will renew your car tag soon.

I am paying extra on (whatever we were discussing) don't worry about it.

I don't know why they shut off the cell phones I paid the bill.

I never got the bill for the water, I guess that's why they shut it off.

I paid all the credit cards off.

We don't owe the doctor's office any money, I paid them off.'

And on and on and on."

- Michelle

On and on is right. Creating financial insecurity in their lives and those closely connected to them is never the abuser's fault. Someone else always fails and didn't do their job, even if that someone is the mortgage company whose only hope is for your payment to arrive.

I don't know about you but being saturated by the communication style that Michelle perfectly outlined would be infuriating. Listening to all of those ridiculous excuses would cause anyone to become annoyed at best. The financially irresponsible person creates life chaos to the point where basic needs are often interrupted, yet they continue to shift the blame on everyone else.

During relationship: "You make more money than me and your parents will help you out; so, you should help me." (I did make more money but I worked two jobs- and my parents did not help me out) "I am working so many hours, so I can take you out but it's expensive and now I am late or can't pay my bills." (He was actually gambling away money and most dates we [went] on I paid)

Marriage: (same guy) "You need to be working; we can't afford anything." (he was gambling) I found $9,000 one day in a drawer and he said grandparents sent money. Later found out he had stolen the money from his job.

Divorce: (same guy) "I am eating noodles and peanut butter sandwiches while you are living a great life."
(I was working two jobs again and he was in Vegas while he said this to me).
"I make more money than you and I can provide a better life for the kids."
(Then took me through a 2-year custody battle; $20,000 later I still have kids but had to defend myself as a good mom, regardless of financial status... and he does have money but refuses to pay the standard child support or any extra for the kids' things)"

- **Kay**

Dating, married, divorced, and the financial abuser was still the same – making demands and telling lies. Did you notice that Kay was working two jobs when they dated, as well as during the divorce time frame? Yet, her financially abusive boyfriend/ex-husband was living in a distorted reality as the victim. In his world, he wanted his then girlfriend to pay for dates because he gambled his money away. Kay's husband wanted her to work more because he was still gambling but now it was with the couple's money. Then, the ex-husband probably didn't want to pay child support (because he returned to gambling his own money away) and tried to further harm Kay by using the family court system against her.

What's the common thread from dating, married, and divorced? A gambling problem that's not addressed and leads to a chronic financial abuser who will stop at nothing to get his way.

2

THREATS

If lies don't work to get financial abusers what they want, they turn to threats next. Instilling fear is a key tactic in the entire operation of economic exploitation. There are as many threats as there are aggressors and I want to cover a few in the genre. What are some of the threats victims hear?

> *I had been out of work for 2 1/2 years due to a cancer diagnosis, surgeries and radiation - I also was having extreme physical, emotional and mental difficulties trying to build up my confidence to work again, and my husband had been paying my bills during this time. Part of my responsibility is board for my horse, I pay $360 a month and I buy her grain and her veterinary and hoof care. My husband gives me $600 a month for food for the household, but I am always short because I have to pay two other bills and the board out of the $600 he gives me. There have been many, many times when he*

has screamed at me that we are short grocery money because of my "--cking horse board!!!" and he has held this over my head many times, threatening to not give me the money for it. My horse is one of my only possessions that is completely about me and for me, I purchased her with money from my family, and she doesn't have anything to do with him. He ALWAYS uses my horse board as leverage over me, never mind that he has many cars and possessions that could be liquidated for bills instead of the only one thing that I have."

– Rhiannon

If nothing is sacred for psychological abusers in general, then this is especially true for those who use money as a weapon. I'm not sure how someone could read Rhiannon's story and not feel for her because of the life circumstances she's faced. What type of detached, void-of-empathy spouse does it take to behave the way he has towards Rhiannon?

Lacking empathy is typical among all financial abusers.

A loving spouse would do whatever it took to ensure that Rhiannon had her horse as a positive outlet in her life during her cancer treatments. Instead, he uses it against Rhiannon as leverage. Why does a spouse need to coerce the person they promised to love and cherish? The constant threat of losing her horse had to create a negative impact on her health and recovery.

Threats against beloved pets is a ploy that abusers utilize because it cuts right into the target's heart. Psychological abusers are on the prowl for what strings they can pull to either keep the victim under their control, or to purposefully inflict emotional distress. It can be hard to imagine that individuals seek ways to harm others and know exactly what they're doing, but unfortunately, it's true. In my book, *Healing from Hidden Abuse*, I cover how to spot these people and more importantly, how to heal if you get caught in their snare.

Told me that there is no way I would make it on my own with our special needs child. Threaten that his parents would pay for his attorney who will be [relentless] in making sure I got nothing out of the divorce, even my child."

– Fooled

Threatening to use the children as a pawn is a favorite tactic for emotional abusers. Is it possible that a perpetrator would pull in his/her parents or other relatives to co-abuse a victim of financial abuse? Absolutely yes. Toxic in-laws are notorious for aligning with their equally as toxic adult child. These families find strength in their numbers and will target the victim spouse and ruin any possibility of success, even going so far as to purposefully destroy the bond between the in-law parent and child.

Why would family members be willing to turn their collective power against an isolated in-law? Unhealthy families need a targeted victim, and there's no one better to play the role of scapegoat than an outsider of the family. It doesn't matter how long the daughter-in-law or son-in-law has been married into the family. Within psychologically abusive extended family systems, there will always be the one who doesn't belong. The in-law is a perfect bullseye for receiving all of the family's focused resentment and dysfunction.

"

When I was a teenager my father said if I did something (can't remember what it was) he would cut me off "without a red cent." I was a really good kid, so it's hard to imagine anything worth that kind of reaction."

- Zia

Imagining a parent using money as a threat against a minor who is still living in the family home may be difficult, but as a therapist who has worked with many youth in this exact situation, I assure you it does happen. Good kids find themselves cut off from all financial support. I know straight-A students and leaders who are winning academic awards and going to school in an affluent area but are secretly living in their cars because poisonous parents cut them off financially. The hidden world of economic abuse is truly all around us.

Toxic parents use money as a way to control because frankly, it works. The idea of being cut off is intensely frightening. Imagine losing all of your credit cards, access to bank accounts, cash, and the locks to your home changed so you can't get in. You instantly have no financial resources other than the gas in your car and no money to use when the tank reaches empty. What would you do? Now imagine you're 16 or 17-years-old. How strong were your problem-solving skills as an adolescent? Probably as good as any of ours were back then – not fully developed, so panic would easily set in.

What could financially abusive parents have to gain from threatening to cut off their own teenager? Free labor is usually what I've seen, such as working at a family business, excessively babysitting younger siblings, or caretaking of a relative. Exploitive parents don't care if they sabotage their kid's development. The parents want their needs met and they see their children as a way to accomplish this goal.

You have no degree and will never be able to afford your kids; you should just give custody to me. You won't be able to stay in this area and if you move I will take the kids away from you. If you leave me I will make sure you never make it."

- Kay

Abusers go for the target's weaknesses to cause as much fear as possible. For Kay, perhaps it was having no college degree and worrying about being able to financially afford being a single parent. I know many people who must weigh the very real financial risk of leaving an abusive relationship. What happens if these individuals haven't been in the workforce for years because they stayed home with their kids or had an extended period of unemployment? Returning to work and making enough money to be self-sufficient often feels like an enormous deficit to overcome to find freedom. As a counselor, this is probably the number one issue I see as to why so many people delay leaving a hostile, if not dangerous, home environment.

Kay's abuser not only tried to make her feel inadequate about her ability to make money, but also went right to the point and told her she should relinquish custody of her children. Give up her right to be their mother. The message is crystal clear and diabolic.

The abuser even covers any future attempts that Kay might make to better her independent financial outlook. If she tried to move to an area she could afford more easily, the toxic parent would use that as grounds to fight for full custody of the children. Would this individual have been successful in the courts? We don't know, maybe, maybe not. The threat is often enough to stop a target of financial abuse from taking key steps to set healthy boundaries. What if the abuser successfully took Kay's kids away from her? That may not be a risk she was willing to gamble on and I doubt anyone could blame her.

> *When I asked for divorce - "I have a friend who is divorced, and you know what? He only pays $12 a month in child support for his ex-wife, and they have 2 kids together!" Whenever he tried to break my phone - if I asked him - "please don't break my phone! Give it back" he would say - 'it is not your phone, it's mine, because I pay for it!!'"*

- Sephora

Economic abusers know how to rig the child support game. They often collect friends who live life in a similar dubious fashion. They share tips and tricks of how to get out of being a responsible adult. Paying $12 a month in child support with two kids is disgraceful, yet happens more frequently than most people realize.

Sephora knew her spouse well enough to know he'd follow through on trying to get out of his moral obligation to care financially for his children. She also knew that he'd have the support of the $12-a-month-guy and I'm betting that father probably knew a shady lawyer who would help Sephora's spouse pay as little as possible. That's what happens. Deadbeat parents are friends with other deadbeat parents and they exchange referrals for services like an attorney. I've witnessed this first-hand. Toxic people have a way of finding one another to help support their often illegal, backdoor deals. Knowing that your spouse will try to leave you with the full financial responsibility of raising the kids is part of what survivors must consider when deciding to leave. If we could ask Sephora, I'm sure she'd agree.

As a teenager, my mother would threaten to deny me access to the car but make it my responsibility to ensure I got my sister and myself to school every day. She guilted about every dime she spent on me, but she ran up huge credit card debt buying things for herself. When I was little she [threatened] to send me to live with my father, who I hadn't seen in years. As a college student she threatened to throw me out of the house on breaks if I didn't pay her money."

- Annie

Toxic mothers. They're worthy of a whole book of their own. Annie carried the burden for both herself and her sister and was clearly sabotaged by their mom's erratic threats. Why would a mom insist that her daughter drive but then make that responsibility hard to deliver on? Some parents need to see their children fail. It may be challenging for a healthy individual to wrap their mind around, but there are parents out there who enjoy the game of setting their kids up in impossible situations. If you've had the misfortune of growing up in the sort of environment where nothing is as it seems, you know exactly how this feels. The effects of growing up in an emotionally unstable home can have a lasting impact well into adulthood. The good news is that healing is possible.

Annie was guilted for the things she needed or wanted as a teenager yet mom spent freely on herself. This isn't hard to picture, is it? We may have all known someone in our life who spent excessively on themselves but nickel and dimed those around them. This is nothing but a power move. The financial abuser wants to flaunt their ability to splurge on themselves while causing others to go without. This creates the ultimate Cinderella story, regardless of gender. Men are known to play this game as well. They may collect toys while the rest of the family worries about asking for money for basic needs.

> *He constantly threatened to go to the church and have me reprimanded for not submitting to him. He threatened to take the car from me while I was at work, leaving me stranded. He threatened to take what little money I had access to and deny me even that."*
>
> **- Annie**

Threats of a smear campaign go hand-in-hand with both spiritual and financial abuse. Annie's husband tried to keep her under his financial control by threatening to bring in the church leaders to back him up as the head of the household and call her out for her lack of submission to his abusive ways. A smear campaign can be devastating to the target. The abuser spreads lies among the couple's family, friends, and community.

If Annie's husband did follow through on his threat to come and take the car while she was at work, how embarrassing would it be for her to walk out at the end of the day and the car be gone? What would she say to her co-workers and supervisor? This situation would've been a passive form of a smear campaign. Co-workers at Annie's office might start looking at her differently because clearly, there's "trouble at home." Maybe Annie needed and wanted to maintain a professional image at work and having her irrational husband come and take her car from the parking lot would have caused the dysfunction to bleed over into her work life. Like any survivor of abuse, she probably tried hard to hide that things at home were less than desirable.

When we're feeling financially strapped as it is, having an abuser threaten to gain control over those limited resources can be very scary. Annie knew her financial situation was tenuous. The abuser's threats just added to the feeling of insecurity. Would he have taken the little she had and denied her access to even that? If we've learned anything so far in our journey, I think we both know the answer is a resounding yes.

> *When I said I wanted to go back to school and start a career: "You're the luckiest woman in America because you get to stay home with your kids. All you care about is yourself!" When I okayed a car repair without his permission, and then pointed out it was unfair that he needed to approve my decisions: "Just call me God. I own you. I am YOUR God."'*

- Rachel

Yes, people like Rachel's spouse do exist and say things like, "I am your God." Unbelievable, but true. The arrogance of abusers should never be taken lightly. Grandiosity is the root of someone saying they are another person's god. There is a misconception that psychological abuse is rooted in insecurity and is an attempt to overcompensate for feelings of inadequacy. That simply isn't true. Grandiosity and insecurity do not go together and are polar opposite character traits. Because he believed that he was better than Rachel, he didn't want her making independent decisions even as simple as a car repair. Rachel clearly wasn't viewed as an equal partner in her household. She had to ask for permission to make household economic choices.

Rachel's abuser didn't hide his belief about his role in her life. He saw himself as her god. He said so himself. Psychological abusers frequently tell on themselves. By this, I mean they reveal exactly who they are and how they think. Victims of abuse will often laugh off these sorts of bizarre statements as having been a joke or something odd said in the moment. However, minimizing an abuser's words is very dangerous because we fail to see the risk that's clearly right in front of us.

Financial abusers want life on their terms. What benefit did Rachel's spouse have by keeping her at home and discouraging her career development? Some of us may want to believe that he felt having a stay-at-home mom was best for his kids, but in the context of economic exploitation, Rachel's world was being controlled. This becomes even more clear when she can't make simple daily decisions without her "God's" approval. He said so himself, didn't he?

Bribed my children with money and things when we got into arguments. I was leaving him one time, had the kids

71

loaded in the car and he comes to the car with newest pair of Jordan tennis shoes and says "your mom is leaving me but I thought I would give you these" then of course they start begging me to stay."

- Joni

Kids and teens often miss the subtle lies when they are being manipulated by a toxic parent. Normal developmental stages haven't been reached that help decipher layers of meaning within conversations. Rather than seeing the obvious game that you and I do in Joni's story, her children saw dad being nice. This tactic caused Joni's kids to believe she was the one who could solve the tension in the family. That's precisely the plan of Joni's financial abuser. He actually wasn't being very subtle with the sudden presentation of the new, coveted shoes. Where were the shoes before Joni loaded the kids into the car to leave the family home? Why did he wait to give them to the children? Is it possible that Joni's husband had them put away somewhere so he could present them as needed for bait with the kids? Yes. This level of pre-planning and deception is commonplace for psychological and financial perpetrators.

In this story we see the effective use of triangulation. All parents have heard that putting children in the middle damages their innocent loyalty to each parent, whether deserved or not. At a core level, poisonous parents don't care about their children's well-being. They can't care and still behave in the damaging ways that they do. Joni felt the need to leave her family home and take her children with her. If her husband felt that was a danger to the kids, he should have called the police for assistance. Instead, what does he do? He goes inside and grabs new shoes to bribe the children into pressuring mom to change her mind. That's not a safety issue handled by a concerned dad, but a controlling and manipulative one that put the children smack in the middle while sitting in the car in the driveway of the house, holding new Jordan tennis shoes.

3

BASIC NEEDS

What happens when the lies and threats of financial abuse create the foundation for full exploitation? The abuser either gains overt or covert control over the household income. When this occurs, basic needs start to become scarce, even in households where the income levels do not warrant living in poverty.

> "
>
> *I went for a long time without buying anything for myself. I wore the same pajamas until they fell apart. I wore one bra for four years. I wore the same pair of sneakers for six years. If it was for the kids and he deemed it worthy, he'd give me the money for it. But for me, if I wanted something I was going to have to earn it from him, usually with sex."*
>
> **- Ashley**

Sex as a bargaining tool for basic needs. Does sexual exploitation happen in established relationships? Ashley just confirmed what we know to be true. Sexual coercion, and therefore lack of true consent, is often found in emotionally and psychologically abusive relationships. Financial abuse sets the victim up to be so in need of basic items like a clean bra and shoes, that giving in to the exchange of sex for goods seems like the only option. Ashley's abuser controlled the household funds and therefore was in the position to demand she "earn it from him."

If Ashley's partner gave the nod of approval, she could receive money from him to buy items for their kids. What happened when he didn't believe the items were necessary, but Ashley did? My guess is that the kids went without the items and Ashley was put in a voiceless position. Ask any parent who's a victim of financial abuse what their greatest heartache has been, and many will tell you it's not being able to provide for their children.

> *After filing for divorce, ex-husband discontinued paying my credit card bill (he was the sole income provider), discontinued adding money into our marital account, and left me with no choice but to live in my parents' basement for a month with*

*my three young children, having to
ration groceries and gas (he has
an average yearly salary of $800,000
while he resided in our $900,000
home by himself) until we were able to
get a hearing in front of the judge
to get orders for him to release marital
funds and order child/spousal support."*

- Melanie

Melanie was rationing groceries and gas while living in her parents' basement with their three young kids, and her financial abuser was living alone in their luxury home. Not just his home, but legally Melanie's home, too. That, right there, is a clear picture of financial abuse. The absolute imbalance of access to economic stability is a lightning rod of clarity regarding this type of harm.

How did her husband justify cutting off not only Melanie, but also his own children from their substantial household finances? From what I know about abusers' patterns, they believe their own lies. They then act out with toxic behaviors based on a world that exists only in their head. The abusers often create situations where they portray themselves to be the "real victim" and then feel justified in whatever harmful actions they take - even if this includes having their own kids as collateral damage to their selfish behaviors.

> *I budgeted constantly to make ends meet. If the children needed new shoes, sport club fees, gifts to take to a birthday party it was excruciating. We lived in a high socio-economic area and the children attended expensive private schools, but I always turned down invitations to dinners etc. because I could not afford to go. My close friends knew if they wanted to meet me for coffee they would have to pay. My children would not tell me they had grown out of their shoes or [clothes] to protect me."*

- Jill

Hidden financial abuse is taking place all around us. That includes in what would be considered affluent neighborhoods. My counseling practice is in an area of Texas that's frequently included in "Richest Towns in America" or "Most Affluent Neighborhoods in the U.S." lists. As a seasoned counselor in this community, I've been granted full access to hear the real stories of hidden abuse in all its forms, including severe economic exploitation within high socio-economic communities.

Wealth is not a safe-guard against manipulation and control through money. On the contrary, I've found that the higher the income bracket, the more hidden the economic abuse becomes. Behind the high-end façade of beautiful homes, manicured lawns, private schools and nice cars, families are subjected to absolute control and dominance by the one holding the purse strings. Just ask Jill and her children. When their shoes became too small, they didn't want to burden their mom by telling her. How many days did her kids arrive at the front door of their private school with shoes that hurt their feet because they had outgrown them?

Why would a parent bother paying for a private school but not clothes that fit their growing children? Many affluent financial abusers agree to the outward trappings of wealth so they can keep up with their business associates and neighbors and look like they belong in the elite world of luxury. It's not uncommon at all for abusers to have millions in the bank and their spouses and kids are scrambling to get their basic needs met and keep the public family illusion going.

> *My spouse removed all the money from our checking account. I wasn't able to buy my feminine products. I had to reach out to my mother for help."*
>
> **– Penny**

When your family member is involved in an economically exploitive relationship, the concept of secondary trauma comes into play. I can only imagine the despair Penny's mom felt when she received what was probably a tearful call or visit about how bad life had become for Penny in her marriage. Secondary trauma can occur for loved ones like Penny's mom. The anger, hurt, and disappointment are all very real for the extended family. Penny's mom may have never liked her daughter's spouse, or maybe she realized that he was an abuser around the same time that Penny did. Either way, family members can be deeply impacted by witnessing their loved one being mistreated. The feeling of helplessness can be overwhelming, especially if the loved one returns to the abuser.

Pause and take in Penny's story for a minute – not being able to buy feminine products because the person who was supposed to love her cleared out every last dime from their marital account. Didn't even leave enough for the basics. Did Penny's spouse stop to think that taking all the money would leave her unable to meet her own needs? Maybe. Maybe not. What we do know is that her spouse cleared out the money and she had to share that news with her mom to get help buying feminine products. If you've ever wondered if economic exploitation is humiliating to the target, the answer is yes.

"I was a stay at home Mom with triplet daughters without a car for 11 years. One of my daughters was born with a congenital heart defect, so not having a vehicle to take her to the doctor if anything came up was very scary, but he could always justify why we couldn't get another vehicle. Usually he'd say we don't have the money, because he's the only one working...he is so good at making it my fault and making me feel guilty for the things we "couldn't afford." However, he always had the money for his paintball, frisbee golf, and every other expensive hobby of his."

- Pam

Upon first reading Pam's story, one might think that her spouse was working hard for his family and just couldn't afford an additional car for Pam to take her medically fragile daughter to the doctor if needed. A lot of families make sacrifices so one person can stay home with the kids. As the primary breadwinner, Pam's husband needed the car to get to work, right? Where her story shifts is in the last sentence. He "always" had money for his expensive hobbies. Ah. Now things look a bit different.

No longer do we see Pam's husband as noble for taking on the full financial weight of caring for the family. We see that spending choices were part of why Pam didn't have a car for 11 years. That's not one or two years while a young couple establishes their financial footing. Going 11 years of spending on yourself and not getting a second car, even though it would've been prudent for safety reasons, is a clear choice on behalf of Pam's husband.

Why didn't he want her to have the freedom that comes with transportation? There are many possibilities and Pam doesn't share the exact reason, but based on how toxic people operate, it must have benefited him in some way. Pam being immobile at home all day meant he had full control over her schedule and knew exactly where she

84

was while he was at work. The other possibility was that it just didn't matter to him. He had a car. He had hobbies. Psychological abusers really are that self-serving. Their lack of compassion can be mind-boggling at times. Again, we don't know the exact reason why Pam didn't have a car for so long, but I assure you it wasn't because they couldn't afford to buy one.

> *Everything.... Even when I asked her if I could get myself something expensive. Like a new pair of shoes or shirt she would say ok. Then when she became physically abusive she would always throw it in my face of what I bought. And I had to agree with her or face being assaulted again."*

- Mark

What basic needs did Mark go without? His answer is everything. He also brings to light that, yes, women can be physically abusive too. The fear associated with being harmed can also be woven into being economically

85

controlled. We must destroy the stereotype that women cannot do damage to their partners. Mark isn't alone in having experienced this in his relationship. Toxic women are just as capable as their male counterparts of causing bruising, bite marks, scratches, welts, broken bones, burns, and so on. We have this myth that men are bigger in size, so they can't be physically abused because they can defend themselves. There are many reasons men don't engage in what's known as mutual combat by physically fighting back.

The shame associated with being a man in a physically abusive relationship is hard to put into words. Add the financial control on top of the threats of physical harm, and most men in this situation have absolutely no one to talk to about the hidden abuse. How does one even start that conversation with their friends? I can tell you, they typically don't. Men need the emotional support to leave an abusive relationship as much as women do. They deserve to have society understand the brainwashing techniques that are associated with psychological abuse equally apply to men as well.

"*Electric was shut off a couple of times. Gas was shut off so that we had no hot water. Had to heat water in microwave or shower with cold water to bathe. Any and all debts just ignored. Hardly any money to buy clothes for our children.*"

– Cynthia

Financial mismanagement leads to poverty. This isn't shocking news to anyone, but what may not be known is that when one person is economically exploitive, the quality of life for everyone involved is deeply impacted. It's impossible to be financially unhealthy and not have it seep into the rest of your life. There are many reasons someone may become grossly irresponsible with money to the point that they're unable to keep the lights on and hot water running. Cynthia told us all debt was also ignored. That's a key point to zero in on.

Sometimes financial abuse occurs because the person in control is severely depressed and stops managing normal functions of life. From what Cynthia shared with us, we don't know if that was the case for the person who economically abused her and her children. I do know that non-stabilized mental health issues can contribute to being so overwhelmed that severe poverty and money mismanagement are the byproducts.

> *In a time of unemployment due to a layoff, we paid tithe over everything else even when I had to rework food for our family. The couple times I chose not to pay the tithe and pay the electricity bill or rent instead, I hid it from my husband out of shame and fear. And then when we got blessed with a check of provision from a source, I told my husband about not tithing and we both made the fear-driven decision to put that check toward "paying back the tithe to our church" instead of using it to keep our family afloat. It was a terrible time and just steeped in fear that came directly from the pulpit."*

– Babette

Messages from the pulpit or individual pastoral meetings that create fear and guilt qualify as spiritual abuse. Plain and simple. Babette and her family were taught to give to the church beyond their means to adequately care for their family. What would cause someone to write a check to their church rather than pay their electricity bill or ensure they had housing? Trauma-inducing fear of displeasing God or even making him specifically angry at them. Babette and her husband lived in the confines of spiritual and financial exploitation and were willing to follow the directives of the leaders they trusted.

As someone who has been a part of church communities for well over two decades, I know for a fact that teaching about giving to the church ranges from give what you feel, all the way to church leaders telling their congregation members that they are welcoming a curse on their entire life if they don't give a specific percentage to that specific church. Cursed. That's a very scary prospect for someone who sincerely believes God is actively guiding and shaping their daily life. The fear that Babette must have felt balancing the needs of her family and not wanting to welcome God's wrath must have been completely crushing at times.

89

Many times it was a choice of giving her money for drugs or food for me. I let her use my car when she had no license to drive to her connection, but she would go to her "friends" house and use drugs there."

- R

Drug dependency often leads to financial harm for those connected to the addict. Maintaining a close connection with someone who struggles with dependency or addiction and not have it taint your own life can be very difficult. Our love and care for those entrapped in addiction will cause economic hardship if we fail to do the hard work of learning and establishing clear boundaries.

R probably thought helping her out was the correct short-term solution. Helping was the little bit of plaster to keep the whole dam from breaking and washing away everything that was important to R. Also, people who are controlled by a substance have a way of relentlessly pushing until they get their way. At some point R must have felt helpless trying to fight the addiction's pull on the person he cared about. We may have a hard time relating to R's dilemma between choosing food or giving her money for drugs. That seems like an easy choice. Yet, if R thought that giving her the money meant she might stay alive one more day, then giving up food seemed worth the exchange.

We went go-carting with our children. An accident happened and another go-cart crashed into me and landed on top of my cart, crushing my hand on the wheel. I told my husband that I thought it might be broken, but he insisted it was just bruised. We didn't have medical insurance and I'm sure he just didn't want to spend the money on medical care. 3 months down the line, it still had not healed properly and I finally was able to get it x-rayed. It had been broken in three places and luckily had fused together where I still had function."

- Joy

He insisted it was just bruised. What formal training led to Joy's abuser believing he had the adequate knowledge to inform her she didn't need medical care? I would bet money he had absolutely no medical education or work history because he got his diagnosis wrong. He arrogantly declared it was a bruise and Joy needed to suck it up and stop complaining that a go-cart landed on her.

A certain category of psychological abusers positions themselves in the world as the end all, be all of knowledge they don't possess. Their arrogance leads to neglect, such as Joy not having her hand properly cared for after breaking it in three places. Her abuser assumed in his infinite wisdom that he could determine she didn't need to spend the money by going to get it looked at by a real doctor.

Financial abusers will cut corners on everyone but themselves. I have a strong suspicion that if it had been his hand that had been injured, he would've been at the first medical clinic he could find. That's how it works in the world of financial abuse. The double standard is staggering.

> *As a result of life-long financial abuse from my narcissistic family, I've never owned my own home, never bought a new car, and don't have as much as most of my peers. I still struggle with money issues because I learned that money will enslave and trap you. My N [narcissistic] parents used money to chain their children to them and choked us with their apron strings."*

- Sandy

Feeling left behind by their peers is a common experience for those who grow up in a toxic family. This happens because normal developmental stages aren't adequately reached due to the dysfunction within the home environment. Growth is slowed down to a crawl when chaos is the norm. Flourishing as a child and adolescent without healthy parenting is very hard. As adults, many of us have had to educate ourselves in the areas we were neglected as kids.

Sandy can look around at her now-adult peers and see that she has missed some of the milestones that our culture says are markers for successful entry into adulthood. She poetically put it best that her parents used money to chain their children and choked them with their apron strings. Sandy is fully aware of how her upbringing negatively influenced her own relationship with money. We often will drag the habits and behaviors from our childhood into our own lives long after we have left our parents' home. Taking control of what we have missed and giving ourselves the freedom to learn as adults is the only way to leave behind a harmful parent's legacy in our life.

> *His contribution of $200 a week wouldn't cover the gas for his car and the food he ate, so I actually had to run the family solely on my pay."*

- 3 strikes

Doing very little but wanting a lot of credit. If you've ever known an adult who behaves like a bratty teenager, this tactic will come as no surprise. These men and women love to give minimal effort but want maximum kudos.

95

Heaven forbid you call them out on their crumbs of effort because then you'll get the typical "nothing I do is ever good enough for you" routine. It's not that nothing is ever good enough, it's that doing the least amount possible is not good enough.

3 strikes took on the full brunt of carrying the family because Mr. $200-a-week-guy was comfortable with having someone else care for him and his kids. When asked, he probably would puff up his chest and tell you all about how he takes care of his family. Living in a delusion is a bright red flag that you might be encountering a covert abuser. Their perception of reality and actual reality are very out of touch. This is especially dangerous because being out of touch with financial truths has devastating consequences for those living in the real world.

> I had pneumonia and he refused
> to take me to the doctor. I had
> to walk there. He refused to pay
> for my prescriptions for said
> pneumonia and insisted the pharmacist
> call my doctor for a cheaper drug.
> He refused to carry health insurance,
> luckily my doctor took payments.
> I was so ashamed and embarrassed
> by him my whole marriage. It got
> to the point he refused to buy me
> food, or very little. I ate canned
> green beans as it was the cheapest
> thing I could come up with that I
> would eat. I hadn't had new clothes
> in 6 years, then he would complain
> about how I dressed. He accused me of
> using "too much" toilet tissue."

- Linda

Complained that she used too much toilet tissue. Now I have heard it all. Linda was married to a man who didn't care about the quality of her life. How do I know this? He demonstrated a complete and total disregard for her access to necessary medical care or having adequate healthy food. What would cause a husband or wife to completely turn financially against their spouse? Disdain and contempt. When these two qualities become cemented within a marriage, all sorts of horrendous behaviors emerge.

You might have noticed that he didn't allow her to spend money on clothes but then was disparaging about her appearance. We see this frequently in relationships where money is a form of control. The target receives the abuse from two different angles. Their access to money is controlled to the point where they're unable to meet their own needs, and then the abuser mocks and shames them for it. This is the ultimate game of set-up.

> *I went many days without food. He would over eat and eat my portion of food. It got to the point the kids and I hid food in my son's bedroom closet because we knew my husband wouldn't go in his room."*

– Brooke

Abusers and food. This is a noteworthy sub-category of harm. People who control through money sometimes like to hoard food for themselves. Their absolute selfish nature comes out through the control and access of food. Some will keep only the "good food" for themselves. Others will eat treats right in front of children and get angry when the kids are rightfully frustrated.

Brooke and her children developed a coping skill and solution by hiding food from the economic abuser. Survivors of chronic mistreatment will come up with their own tricks to get their needs met. Individuals who financially harm others will use the items that money can buy as a tool of control, food being just one of them.

While I worked a full-time job he worked part-time at a pizza delivery place. His contributions consisted of paying for internet/cable and on occasion for groceries and gas.
I had little left over for even myself. I can remember his favorite thing to say was "you got this right?" He knew how much it bothered me and what my paychecks covered expense wise. Post break up he refuses or attempts to refuse to pay the court ordered child support.

I almost had to foreclose on my house. I barely had money for groceries and necessities for me and our two small children. Our youngest had to wear a medically necessary contact that out of pocket can run around $200 just for one. He ignored my request for help to cover the cost. If it weren't for my support system being there I'm sure I would have lost my home amongst other things."

– BJ

You got this right? No, she doesn't "got this" by herself. That statement creates a set-up where BJ has only two options. She could say she doesn't have it all and the financial exploiter would likely use guilt or embarrassment to question why she can't manage it on her own. It seems irrational that a person who doesn't plan to take care of adult commitments himself would guilt BJ, but that's what typically happens within these types of relationships. The second option could be for BJ to not open the door for his displaced judgement and carry the burden by herself. Either way, BJ loses this game and the financial exploiter knows it.

4 CRIMES

As economic exploiters cut corners for their own gain, their behaviors frequently cross the line and are not only abusive, but illegal too. The disregard for other people, societal moral norms, and the law cannot be underestimated. Their internal ethical compass is defective, so we must never default to them as a gauge of determining right from wrong. Their viewpoint is skewed by the absolute singular vision of meeting their own needs.

When times were tough, he'd ask for my diamond wedding ring so he could hock it. I'd have to give it to him because I was a stay at home mom and there was no food. I did this three times. He always got it back for me. The fourth time, I told him it had no meaning anymore and so I wouldn't wear it. I put it in my purse. When I went to look for it, it was gone. I asked him if he had seen it. He said no and spent an hour looking for it with me. It came out about 10 years later that he had hocked it and didn't get it back."

- Erin

He spent an hour looking for the wedding ring with her. An hour. That isn't just a quick breeze through a couple of rooms, but an hour of searching that would have included moving furniture, pillows, blankets, and so on. He pretended to be equally concerned about the disappearance of his wife's wedding ring, but withheld the hidden financial secret that he'd hocked it and kept the money for himself. While he was looking, he knew the truth. This behavior starts to hit on the malicious spectrum.

The lengths that exploiters are willing to go to and keep the charade continues to astound me. They have no problem whatsoever looking you right in the eye and lying. These folks will frequently use tears and eloquent words of remorse, when later you come to find out it was all an act. The theatrical antics of psychological abusers are absurd. It would be funny if their farce wasn't so damaging to the people around them.

He attempted to withdraw and hide $60,000 during our divorce proceedings."

- CC

Keep a close watch on all the common funds leading up to a separation and through the stages of a divorce. I've heard numerous stories of financial abusers moving large amounts of money out of joint accounts, even when they've been advised by their attorney or the court not to do so.

Have you noticed that the rules you or I must govern ourselves by somehow seem to not apply to these individuals? Toxic people live within their own set of rules and the hardest part is that many times, they don't get their hand slapped for being shady. They often get away with it. Why is this? Savvy financial abusers know exactly how to skirt the laws in just a way that it doesn't come back and land in their lap. This is all part of the game for those who have the financial sophistication to excel at being a criminal.

"He filed our taxes electronically and when the refund came in had it deposited into an account I did not have access to. Two years later, only two months after our divorce was finally final, I found out he had filed incorrectly and the refund that was received was about $3,500 over what it should have been. Because we were still married, although I never saw a cent of it and it didn't go to any household needs, I was still liable for half of it and therefore it was taken out of my personal refund that year."

- Kimberlee

Being legally married creates all sorts of entanglements that most people never think about until the tentacles of an abuser start to constrict them. Many people are unaware that the person they pick as a partner can and will have serious implications on their own financial liabilities. In some states, the laws are crystal clear that debts are the responsibility of both spouses, even if only one ran up the debt during the marriage.

Kimberlee shows us here that tax liability and filing correct tax returns also fall into this joint ownership category. Many abused spouses have no idea what was put on the yearly tax returns and are told to sign them regardless. There are some individuals who have been able to file an Innocent Spouse Relief form with the IRS if they find out that their ex or current spouse should be solely liable for the tax burden.

> *He forged my name on a loan document and his friend notarized it; I understand after I filed for divorce that he has 2 sets of accounting records for his*

business (this was a threat to me also because I'm a CPA, but I never touched his business records intentionally)"

- Jen

Jen knew intuitively to not touch her husband's business books. She may not have received proof until after the divorce that he was keeping two sets of accounting (which is illegal by the way), but she was wise to not have any of her fingerprints on his sketchy business accounting. Why? She could be held professionally liable for the illegal activity conducted within the business, even if she wasn't fully aware of all of the dealings. Most professional organizations don't care for the "I didn't know" alibi, despite it being true in Jen's case. Her husband kept key financial information away from her. However, unless Jen had a paperwork trail of proof showing she was intentionally misled, it's likely she might have been sanctioned or possibly had her ability to work in the industry revoked. Let's not forget any criminal cases that might have developed from an investigation into her husband's business dealings. Again, who we partner with in both marriage and business can have a devastating impact on our lives.

> *Pornography, child pornography. He had credit cards I was unaware of to pay for images. He also purchased equipment to make his own pornography. Money was being funneled to this illegal activity while I was being accused of 'overspending'."*
>
> **- Shana**

The world-wide illegal sex industry receives an alarming amount of money that originates from the bank accounts and lines of credit from our next-door neighbors, close college friends, friendly co-workers, family members, your child's youth leader at church, and even spouses who we would never suspect. This isn't an epidemic happening on the other side of the world – it's right here in our towns. This under-belly world in society shouldn't be considered out of sight, out of mind. Minor sex trafficking and pornography is an abuse hidden in plain sight. Without the financial resources of people like Shana's partner, the entire industry would collapse.

While Shana's spouse was spending the couple's money on sexually abusing children, he also was complaining about her overspending. This makes me wonder how those conversations went. Did she return from the grocery store with too many snacks and he decided to grumble about the excessive bags of potato chips in the pantry, while he had images that he paid for of children being used for sex on his computer? Seriously. High-spectrum financial abusers lack insight into their own twisted way of viewing money and how it is used.

> *Invested in a business with our counselor of 8 years behind my back and found out he was having a relationship w/her."*
>
> **- Marie**

I had to read this response twice when I came across it while going through the research data. Marie's partner not only invested in a business with their counselor but was also in a relationship with this same counselor. There are layers of issues with what took place in Marie's world.

No counselor should be talking to you about financial investments with them. Period. If this happens, please protect yourself and find another therapist. You may also choose to alert the licensing board for that particular therapist. We're governed by many rules, laws, and regulations regarding our interactions with clients. Financial intertwining is never acceptable and falls into the dual relationship category. If co-mingling business interests isn't allowed, you can imagine that having a romantic relationship with a current client is explicitly unacceptable. A professional therapist can and should lose their license for having a romantic relationship with a client.

> "Check kiting, which resulted in multiple [closed] bank accounts (including the children). Forging my signature to get cable (which I didn't agree to). Writing bad checks. Taking money that the kids earned from their children's [accounts]."
>
> - J

In the research I conducted for this book, the topic of check kiting came up several times as a common practice among some economic abusers and financial criminals.

This practice involves writing a check from Account A and depositing it into Account B, making Account B's balance temporarily go up. Then, other items clear Account B and are paid because of the new higher balance. However, Account A never had enough funds for the check written, but it may take a few days for the bank to get an insufficient funds notice on Account A. This is why some banks will put a hold on larger checks and wait for it to clear from the original account – Account A in my example.

J's abuser ran this scam using her kids' money and bank accounts. Nothing is sacred or off limits for a toxic person. I honestly don't get it. Running a check kiting scam and stealing from your own children seems to take a lot more effort than just getting a real job and being an adult. The energy that financial exploiters use to harm others could be put towards healthy endeavors like supporting themselves, instead of leeching off those in their family. Even the kids.

Pretended to have power of attorney with my divorce lawyer and conducted actions in my divorce without my knowledge until I got a $6,000 bill, canceled my utilities without authority, damaged my car so it would not run, broke my windows, excavated dirt from under my home, called boyfriends and employers repeatedly anonymously and attempted to get me isolated from people and employment."

– Jane

Jane was financially abused by a parent. Now go back and re-read what she shared with us. Maintaining and protecting a high quality of life can be very difficult when you have your own mother or father behaving the way Jane's did. We don't know why Jane's parent had chosen to have absolutely no boundaries or would want to intentionally harm her. From a psychological perspective, I can come up with a few possibilities, and jealousy would be my first guess. Few people go to this much trouble to harm their own adult child without having a streak of hatred and loathing. As we go through life, we should be aware that parents like Jane's do exist and cause tremendous financial heartache for their adult children. If you have a friend who shares a story with you about his or her out of control parents, don't immediately assume the friend is exaggerating or being paranoid. Remember Jane and the fact that some parents attempt to sabotage their adult children from succeeding in life.

Identity theft by withdrawing children's 529 accts that were in my name. Used our son's name and debit card for Ashley Madison dating site. Told car insurance agent he was my fiancé when getting car insurance in my name without my knowledge. Check kiting. Tax fraud. Lied on tax returns to get the most refund possible for [multiple] years. Never paid taxes on the withdrawals on the 529's accts which I'll be responsible for if audited."

– Charlene

Used their son's name and debit card for an online account created for married individuals who are looking to have an affair. Do I need to say anything else?

"
He loved insurance and medical fraud. His ex would provide medical care receipts for him to reimburse her and he would use them like he had paid the bills himself and got reimbursed by his insurance flex plan. I owned my house but the home insurance was in his name. He kept telling me to make claims and then the payments would have been mailed directly to him. He tried but I was able to contact the company and get the policy cancelled."

– Gem

As a therapist who specializes in trauma recovery, I've heard a lot from victims, but not the financial abuse scam of using the receipts provided by the ex to re-file through their own insurance coverage. Clever and highly illegal.

Not only was the ex-spouse used by this abuser, but so was Gem because he pulled her into his toxic world of attempting to get her to file claims on the house so he could take the money. We know this financial abuser had multiple victims which is typically how they operate. Seldom does an abuser single out one victim. They may attempt to make it look like their behaviors are confined to the current relationship, but when we dig deeper, a trail of exploitation follows these individuals.

Reading Gem's story makes me wonder if he willingly set up the home insurance in his own name for the purpose of running this scam. Premeditated economic abuse. Gem was smart to put a stop to it. I don't know how long ago this occurred, but I do know that insurance laws have become tighter because of exactly what Gem's abuser did to her. Apparently, there were many people trolling this same scam.

> *He would sell me for the sexual use of others. He would drive constantly [without] a license, drive drunk, sell drugs. Steal license plates to put on our cars. Not file taxes and when he*

*did, lied as to the actual income. Paid
me under the table so he wouldn't
have to declare my income, claimed me
as a [Dependent]...even after we
were divorced."*

– Gypsy

We start Gypsy's story with the most obvious form of financial exploitation and abuse, serving as a pimp for his own wife. We should pause here for a moment, let the reality of this set in, and not for a second judge Gypsy. We don't know the exact life path she took to end up entangled with a high spectrum abuser but as an expert in this field, I assure you it didn't happen overnight.

At the far end of the abuse continuum, brainwashing techniques are used by malignant abusers. There is a parallel process that we can observe when people find themselves engulfed in a highly exploitive relationship and what we see in spiritual or religious cults. No one sets out to join a toxic group, and Gypsy didn't sign up to be sexually used for her husband's financial gain. In the early stages of an encounter with a cult, people think they're joining a friendly group that promises to accept and support them. Likewise, individuals never willingly start an abusive relationship. In both situations, the subtle shifts often go unnoticed until the depth of the calculated control becomes obvious. One day Gypsy realized the path that her brutal husband led her down. We know this because she said his criminal activity continued after their divorce.

5 SABOTAGED

Ask any victim of financial abuse and they'll share their attempts to find freedom from the control, manipulation, and harm. Toxic people will intentionally and cruelly sabotage any steps towards growth and independence. Why do they do this? Abusers like the way life revolves around their needs and demands for control. They won't give those up without a fight.

> *Total chaos with the children at home while I was working. My husband would have fits of rage/bouts of anger at home with smaller children. When I came home children would be in tears. It was hard working while concerned for children's safety."*
>
> **- Mary**

Mary's story is typical of what we would expect within this world of mistreatment. Making the victim fearful that their children could be harmed is a psychological game that malicious people frequently play. Whether it's a perceived harm or actual damage, the sabotaging effect is still the same.

Mary found it difficult to work while the children were at home with their father. Coming home to scared, tearful children confirmed her worries. How was Mary supposed to continue leaving them in the care of a scary dad? Switch genders and the dilemma is still the same. Many fathers feel anxious about leaving for work knowing his children aren't in an emotionally or physically safe environment with their mother. The financial implications of inadequate childcare options are enormous.

I've worked with clients whose entire professional careers were derailed because a toxic partner ruined their ability to be away from home without the kids. The double bind of having children to protect but needing to work full-time is one of the hardest obstacles for victims of financial abuse to overcome.

> *When the church got involved and recognized our marriage as abusive, he gave them large donations from our only savings/retirement/children's college funds and said he was "pre-tithing" for years to come."*

- K

127

Nothing says guilt like delivering a large check just as leadership is starting to put the pieces of the puzzle together. K's husband wasn't even subtle about his bribe to the church leaders. Trying to dress it up as a "pre-tithe" is ridiculous and goes to show his complete lack of creativity. He would have been better to lie and say God told him to give away the family's savings, retirement, and the children's college funds. Instead he used the pre-tithe excuse, which in the church world isn't a real thing.

Are you thinking the same thing I am? Wondering if the bribe worked and there was a sudden shift in how K was treated by the church leaders? Me too. I hope that her husband's gift was seen for exactly what it was. I also wonder how well the family navigated the next financial emergency with no savings, what their retirement plans are, or how the kids will pay for expenses in college. All that money was given to the church so they would side with K's husband and stop looking into their abusive marriage.

> *He's always sabotaging our finances,*
> *so I can't afford to buy anything, and*
> *make sure I can't put away any money*
> *to leave. He will also sabotage our*
> *finances when a huge bill is due...he*
> *goes on a huge spending spree right*
> *before he knows I'm working on paying*
> *off a huge bill. Then he will ask if I got*
> *that bill paid off. If I say no, he acts as*
> *though it's something I'm doing wrong...I*
> *just don't know how to budget money."*

– Pam

Keeping the funds depleted is one tactic of control. We see this with passive abusers, as well as the overt type. If the family finances can be harnessed in a way that there's never quite enough or always a revolving line of new credit debt, then the abuser is able to train the victim to think that finding freedom will never be an option. This tactic works because who can leave without any money? It takes funds to find a new place to live, to move, to hire an attorney, and to put food on the table. Always sabotaging any financial traction is an effective way to keep a target trapped.

Ran up huge credit card debts in my name only. Left me when I was still on maternity leave with 2 small children (one only 9 months) Said to me "look at you now, a single mother on welfare."
Told his new partner very private information about me which she (affair partner) threatened to tell my employer to embarrass me. Borrowed $10,000 off my elderly parents."

- Naisey

Look at you now. The battle cry of shame. Those four words carry so much power within them. Naisey was left by her husband with two kiddos and he turns back and attempts to belittle her for now being a single mom burdened with the credit card debt he ran up. He not only left her with the kids, but the debt too. To add insult to injury, his mistress was willing to threaten the stability of Naisey's employment. This story makes me wonder why some people are so cruel. Who are these people that are void of normal human compassion and willing to sabotage another person's ability to be financially sound for herself and her kids? As uncomfortable as it might make us, we have to come to terms with the fact that some people are dreadful. Their intentions are to harm and they do not care what damage is done.

He took $6,000 of my savings, claiming it was for family expenses when it was in fact to prevent me from hiring a lawyer."

– Keliegh

131

If an abuser is so unhappy being with a certain target, why would they try and stop the victim from hiring a lawyer and leaving them? Because the abuser likes their life and does not want to see things change. Sure they may ridicule, belittle, and in general harass a victim, but at the end of the day, the quality of their life works for them. They enjoy the control they reign over the victim and may also be comfortable with other aspects of their lifestyle together. It may be counterintuitive to see someone trying to keep a partner that they aren't attached to and exploit on a regular basis, but it frequently happens.

> *At this time he is attempting to ruin my professional reputation by telling lies that I am mentally unstable. It has cost me clients and I'm not sure to what extent my business can recover. However, I have downsized, so I am making adjustments to compensate for that sabotage."*
>
> **- Kim**

There are some professions that all you have is your reputation and when an economic abuser sets his or her sights on destroying that, tremendous financial damage can be done. Kim knows her abuser has cost her clients and she's assessing the full scope of the destruction. As a business owner, she is wise to adjust her expenses to her current level of clients to help off-set the harm done to her and her business portfolio.

How does one come back from a business smear campaign? Some situations warrant meeting with the key players within your profession to share how your reputation is being intentionally sabotaged and by whom. This, however, may be a risky move for some social circles and work environments. One of the best ways to combat a smear campaign is to keep doing what you do best. Let the attack on your reputation shrivel up as you stay focused on your strengths and rebuilding. If you feel like you've lost your professional swagger, find ways to get your hustle back. It may mean taking some time to meet with a therapist or seasoned life coach. As they say, the best revenge is living well. Smear campaigns have a way of falling off the radar over time and in the end, the economic abuser will look petty for their attempts to derail your business or career.

> *The first time I caught him it was 100%
> intuition. I had no reason to check
> my safe. But I swear a voice was in [me]
> telling me to. He had replaced $25,000
> worth of gold coins with metal washers.
> He seemed remorseful. Nobody ever
> stole from me before so what did I know.
> We were married one month when
> he stole it."*

- Kat

Catching your spouse stealing from you is a moment that would cause cognitive dissonance for anyone, then add the fact that the theft took place so early in Kat's marriage. It's easy to see why she took the theft as maybe a one-off moment for her husband. He seemed remorseful. In hindsight, he was able to talk his way out of getting caught. From Kat's own words, she said that was the first time she caught him. We can connect the dots that more episodes of spousal theft followed.

"

I believed him when he said he'd take care of me. I had 3 children in 3 years 9 mos. so raising them was intense because of their closeness in age. He always wanted me to be a stay at home mom, whenever I expressed interest in anything, he would say something to the effect that "just be sure dinner is on the table for me." A Realtor friend of mine asked me to go work with her on her team. She thought I'd be great and wanted to mentor me. My kids were in High School at this time, I should have been able to do this. But I knew he would never help with the meals, never help in the kitchen, was cruel and a tyrant to the kids. I couldn't leave to do what I really wanted to do. I also knew there'd be fighting if he came home and a meal wasn't ready because I was off showing a house. Now that I'm finally away from him, and my children are safely away also, I can finally pursue this."

- Vanessa

Angry if dinner wasn't on the table. This is a traditional, patriarchal household expectation that Vanessa's husband held as king of the castle. If I could ask Vanessa, I'd want to know if her husband thought of himself as religious because his tone and demands follow that of a male dominate theology.

For some reason, Vanessa's story reminded me of the time a male senator was arrested in a hotel with a 17-year-old boy and in the video of the arrest, the senator's t-shirt read, "Ephesians 5:22 – Now Go Make Me a Sandwich." Ephesians 5:22 talks about wives submitting themselves to their husbands. Oh, the irony of his arrest while wearing that exact t-shirt. I bet he would have planned his wardrobe differently had he known he was going to get arrested and be on camera in a motel with an underage boy.

Vanessa's husband expected his world and timeliness of his meals to be catered to by his wife. Her ability to start branching out of stay-at-home-mom-land didn't change when her kids reached even high school and may have been driving themselves around town. Why would her husband sabotage her ability to start a real estate career with a trusted mentor? It simply wasn't important to him and might cramp his schedule. Vanessa was viewed as a subordinate to him and her job was to meet his needs. I wonder who has those duties now that Vanessa is free on her own, with her kids, building her real estate business. Maybe he has to make his own sandwich.

> *It took four years to get divorced*
> *because he would not relinquish any of*
> *our joint assets. My attorney stated*
> *that he had structured his assets in*
> *such a way that it was as if he*
> *had known he would divorce me prior*
> *to marrying me. He sent a seven-page*
> *letter detailing all of my previous*
> *sexual experiences as well as other lies*
> *about my mental stability to*
> *my employer after we separated."*
>
> **- Chris**

Sabotage can be years in the making and come in the form of asset structure that solely benefits the abuser. This is especially true if the individual is a financial planner, attorney, or other professional who has knowledge of how to set it up and keep that information from their future or present spouse.

The feeling of betrayal is intense when a survivor of abuse recognizes they've been manipulated all along. This causes their perception of the entire relationship to come into question, and they doubt themselves deep down to their core. As a therapist working with these clients, I frequently remind them that they met a con artist who scammed them. There may have been sporadic warning signs early on, but nothing that would warrant a full retreat from the person. The higher the level of toxicity, the more of the con is hidden. Since psychological and financial abusers have the maladaptive skill set to lie to your face while smiling, recognizing his or her ill-intentions would be very hard to do early in the relationship. Many abusers don't show their true colors until after the wedding when they believe it's too late for the target to back out. One very common thread among psychologically abusive marriages is they all tend to move fast. Meet, date, get engaged, and married quickly. When this takes place, there isn't adequate time to see through the masks of the abuser. They can keep the illusion of normalcy going only for so long and frequently will rush the relationship so the commitment is cemented before they reveal their true toxic nature.

"

I believe I was sabotaged before we even got married. When we were dating, he had me quit my job because the hours made me unavailable in the afternoons and evenings. That was stupid on my part to listen. I thought I could get a better job, but I didn't. He took over my finances, combined our credit cards when we got married. But instead of working together, he completely took over and destroyed my credit to where I couldn't even get a bank account at a local bank. He did this by not paying bills in my name, and only paying bills in his name. I realized this after some items went to collections and I started getting phone calls about delinquent accounts. I was far too trusting, as I am a very honest person. He still denies that he does this on purpose. He calls these [occurrences] "mistakes," but it happened so many times, I lost count."

- Joy

139

The same mistakes don't keep happening. Joy's story illustrates the exact process of someone engulfing and sabotaging their partner financially. His bills were paid, but hers were not. She couldn't get a bank account in her own name because of the damage he had done to her credit. This was most definitely not by accident. We live in a world where our credit score matters. I know some teachers in the area of finance encourage people to go completely off the grid when it comes to credit but for most people, having a good credit score opens doors to financial freedom. Having it impaired causes people to not be able to rent an apartment or house, turn on utilities, or open a bank account. Damaging someone's credit takes their financial feet right out from under them and requires a rebuilding process that we'll explore later in our time together.

"

He's an attorney and wrote an unconscionable prenuptial agreement that I signed just days before our wedding with representation that he hired for me, and I am now learning upon filing for divorce from my current attorney that he has the entire prenup set up so any money he would make during our marriage (millions were made by him) would essentially be considered "separate assets" if we were ever divorced. It didn't matter how long we were married and how much he would make, he would get almost all of the money and I would be left with minute "payouts" i.e. $75,000 under 5 years of marriage, 10 years of marriage only paid $120,000, with a maximum amount of $200,000. He makes $800,000/year. He used it as another way to try to get me not to leave him."

– Melanie

No matter how much money was made during the years of the marriage, Melanie would be given a set amount as a final settlement. Since he made millions, a payout of $75,000 is not even 10 percent of one million. I know for some people, getting $75,000 in a lump payment would be a huge windfall. For comparison purposes, Melanie's minimum settlement after five years of marriage would be the equivalent of one spouse getting $20,000 and the other receiving $2,000. One is getting crumbs compared to the other.

Melanie's attorney husband had someone he hired "represent" Melanie's interests prior to signing the prenup, but clearly this person failed to disclose the true structure of the payouts or else this wouldn't have been shocking news when she filed for divorce. Even after Melanie found out about his bait and switch prenup, her husband tried to use the small payout as leverage to keep her in the marriage. I can envision an abuser saying something similar to, "If you like your current lifestyle, withdraw the divorce petition and you can have access to my money." Basically, using the wealth as a means of puppet strings to be attached to Melanie.

142

Every single time I started to get ahead in my work (which eventually stabilized, but as a series of low income jobs) he'd hit me with another suit to cut off support payments. Back in court. Back paying another lawyer. He lost [every] time. Judge refused to vary the payments. But he blamed me for the costs he had to pay for filing the suit."

- Kathleen

Exes have an uncanny ability to know precisely when you get back on your feet and that's when they pounce again. Many enjoy using the family court system as a means of continued turmoil and harassment. Even though the judge denied Kathleen's ex a change to his payments, he kept on trying. Some people never learn. The kicker is that he tried to turn it around on Kathleen and blame her for his own decision to come back again after failing. It's almost as if he was engaged in magical thinking that this next time, the judge will finally see things from his distorted perspective and agree to lower the payments. But the judge didn't see it that way at all. What an utter and complete waste of energy and time for Kathleen, who was trying to build her financial foundation.

> *As soon as alimony & child support was awarded he "lost" his engineering job. He then would give money here and there from his unemployment. I learned from my kids he was working and he'd deny it. After years of him being in arrears we went back to court so*

arrangements could be made to start paying back the $30,000 he owed me. At this point he was working for himself and I was remarried. He falsified his income and made it look like I had more money than he did. His lifestyle proved otherwise but now I had to pay him child support and it was deducted from the back pay he owed me."

– Jodi

No one believes he actually lost his job at the same time the support was awarded, right? Of course not. He left his job to find work he could hide from the family court. This happens all the time in the world of financial abuse. Ask any dad or mom who has shouldered the full economic burden for their kids because their ex-spouse hid their income and got away with it.

Jodi's ex maintained a lifestyle that proved different than what he was claiming in the financial declarations to the court. We desperately need the family courts to be reformed so parental neglectors can no longer hide their money from their kids, because ultimately that is what's happening. This is true, whether the spousal or child support is being illegally impacted. It isn't about the ex-spouse, but about failing to provide the financial resources possible for their children.

> *He often dropped me off at work in the morning and he would yell at me all the way there. I arrived at work in tears many mornings. I eventually was fired from that job after seven years of service. It is strange, because in the beginning of our relationship, my husband used to tell me that my boss didn't appreciate me and he wouldn't be surprised if he just fired me without warning [someday]."*

– Anne

Psychological abusers refuse to temper their emotional responses when it isn't a good time for the other person. A healthy individual would be willing to assess that arguing with Anne on her way to work might not be the most ideal time and would wait until a more appropriate place to discuss their irritations. Going into work chronically tearful had to impact Anne's productivity and her abuser knew it would. He already started laying the ground-work of doubt in Anne's mind about her boss and the stability of her employment, even though she had been there 7 years. I'm curious as to how long she'd been at her job before she started dating her husband because from reading her story, it sounds like the job came first. If this were true, Anne's job had a bullseye on it for her abuser. Toxic partners set out to sabotage steady employment because they know that with financial stability comes personal independence. That's a threat to the type of controlling relationship a psychologically abusive partner is attempting to establish.

> *I wasn't allowed to have any money [whatsoever]. If I asked I was beaten. I was beaten if I asked for the mail key so I never knew what bills were being put in my name."*
>
> **- Celeste**

Beaten. Physically bruised and injured because you asked for money or the key to the mailbox. This is the truth for many survivors of violence. Little, normal, everyday events like wanting money for basic needs turns into irrational, violent explosions. Celeste couldn't assess what damage was being done to her credit because she wasn't allowed access to it. Her abuser controlled all aspects of her financial well-being or lack of. He had her in an invisible cage and I doubt anyone else noticed. The sabotage ran so deep that I imagine she found it hard to even picture in her mind what it would take to try to get away from the rage and establish her own independent life.

6 TURNING POINT

In every unhealthy relationship, there comes a point where the quality of the connection becomes crystal clear. Victims no longer wonder if something is off or doubt their assessment of the situation. Usually there's a proverbial last straw that brings the picture into painful clarity. That is when a turning point takes place.

> *I was pregnant and I told him that he had to get a job. He looked at me and said "I shouldn't have to do that." I was forced to go back to work shortly after my c-section because we had no money. It was then I realized who and what he was."*
>
> **- Eliza**

Nothing shows us someone's character better than when we're in need of their support and through their free-will, blatantly refuse to help. Eliza's partner clearly showed his sense of entitlement and willingness to have her financially support him. Not only did he show it, he followed through by not stepping up so she wouldn't have to go back to work right after surgery and the birth of their child. This wasn't just a passing thought of why he should be forced to go to work, but the actual value he holds. Why should he have to work? Eliza can do it. I'm not sure where in this man's life experience taught him that it was fine to not work and to exploit your pregnant partner, but I'm thankful Eliza chose to share her story with us because we all need to know these individuals are out there. Consider yourself warned.

> *I started asking him to keep receipts so I could pinpoint why our budget wasn't working. He "forgot" to save them. I opened a separate checking account and was able to have money left at the end of each month instead of being completely out of money or overdrawn."*
>
> **– A**

Great plan. Ask for receipts to track the spending and very quickly, you'll see what level of resistance you get from a financially toxic person. Funny how he kept forgetting. A pattern started to reveal itself and A was smart for creating economic distance. This allowed her the clarity she needed to know it wasn't her behavior that caused the chronic money issues.

Survivors of abuse frequently struggle with blaming themselves for the problems in the relationship and since the abuser likes to blame them too, it can be confusing to find the truth within the vortex of allegations. Using boundaries as a necessary tool helps survivors pinpoint exactly where the responsibility should rest. After A was able to see she was in fact capable of managing the money, I bet it gave her a confidence boost.

Until I left him in 2012 I didn't even know that financial abuse was a recognized pattern of abuse. I knew when he took all the monthly child support I received for my daughter from a previous relationship that his controlling behavior was out of line, that was in about 1990. For more than 20 years I thought that it was just him doing this to me to keep me under his thumb and unable to leave. It was a revelation when I found that I wasn't alone in this type of abuse."

– CC

CC summarized the whole point of writing this book – for survivors to know they aren't alone in this type of abuse. I'll also add that the world needs to know what hidden economic destruction looks, feels, and acts like. When we have a common language and understanding of how financial exploiters and abusers operate, targets will no longer be isolated. Without a general understanding that people intentionally set out to harm those in close proximity to them, targets remain in the shadows with very little support.

By examining the relationships he had had before me, I realized that he had absolutely no responsibility for himself. He sponged off of whatever partner he had at the time, and whenever they would get sick of it, he'd triangulate with other women, use flying monkeys and threats of suicide to gain sympathy. When I started to try and set boundaries, he'd retaliate by cheating, lying, stealing, etc. If I didn't provide food, beer, shelter, cell phone, money, car, he would either find someone who would (usually a woman who he was sleeping with) or he'd try and manipulate his way into getting what he wanted from me. His promises to stop lying, cheating, and stealing from me came with the caveat that I needed to start to trust him and not check up on him anymore. That's when I knew he was only interested in himself and what he could con people out of so he could have the least amount of responsibility for himself as possible. That he never truly intended to love me, provide for me and our daughter (let alone himself), or have any reciprocity in our relationship. Everything was about him."

- Leah

This. A whole lot of this and for days, Leah has captured the turning point perfectly. She came to realize everything was about him.

> *I feel like a prisoner in my own home. There's no mutuality, reciprocity or freedom.*"
>
> **– Penny**

It can be a powerful and devastating moment when we clearly see our life situation for what it is. Penny is right. If she's married to a person who uses money as a weapon, her life will feel like prison. We've already seen how mutuality isn't the goal for those who seek toxic control in their families or places of worship. These connections are riddled with double standards regarding respect and personal responsibility. If we stay in any level of pity for the abuser or denial about how bad the relationship has become, we become our own saboteur. Once we can view our lives with raw honesty, we're then positioned to make lasting changes.

158

"

My pastor's wife encouraged me to get through my training as quickly as possible in order to minimize x's ability to "sabotage" my education."

- El

May God richly bless the spiritual leaders and their co-leader spouses who understand the complexities of hidden abuse and the ways to properly support its victims. El is very fortunate to have healthy, religious mentors in her life. Far too frequently we hear about toxic places of worship and their unwavering, bizarre support for the abusers. We're currently seeing the American Evangelical church show its under-belly regarding the unethical handling of disclosures of abuse and crimes perpetrated by staff pastors and church leaders. This is not breaking news for those of us who are professionals within a faith-based setting. We've heard the stories of abuse survivors being blamed for their mistreatment and given the responsibility to keep quiet about what has happened to them. Their silence was demanded all in the name of protecting the image of the church. If a disclosure did happen, I have worked with

159

counseling clients who were told they had to apologize to their abusive leader for "tempting him to sin." I'm not kidding. The level of pathological distortion and victim-blaming within the church has led to further devastation for many faithful individuals.

El is one of the lucky ones. Her turning point came when she received the support she deserved and needed from her church community. It's hard to describe how meaningful it is for survivors when they're encouraged by their faith-leaders to protect themselves from an abuser. Telling a victim that they are worthy of protection and have a right to speak up about abuse is one of the clearest messages about human value that a pastor or church leader can give to their congregation members.

The final stage for me was realizing the hopelessness of the situation, he would never change and I would have to leave, to protect myself and to model the right behavior to my children in the hopes that my daughter would never marry an abuser and my sons

160

would never marry nor become abusers themselves. Now that I'm out, this is the prayer of my heart for them now."

– Vanessa

Acceptance is an important part of any recovery process. Victims of financial abuse must give themselves time to grieve the figurative death of what they thought the relationship was going to become. Things didn't turn out like they'd dreamed and were promised by the toxic person.

Vanessa was motivated, like many healthy parents, to leave the hate-filled environment so her children would have better role models. This point can't be taken lightly. Our children see and hear more than we give them credit for and it has an impact on their subconscious beliefs about marriage, love, and ability to be loved unconditionally. Divorce is no one's first or easy choice, but sometimes it's the only way to keep children safe.

If anyone tries to tell you that people are casually discarding their marriages, you instantly know they have no idea what they're talking about. As a therapist, I've sat with clients agonizing over the few choices that were left because of the level of harm in the marriage. I have yet to meet a single, healthy client who didn't take ending their marriage with deep levels of pain and trepidation. The only people who end their marriages with little regard are those whose attachments are questionable, and that's usually the abuser.

> *When the money was magically available when he no longer felt like I was definitely going to leave him."*
>
> **- Fooled**

One of the most liberating times for an abuse survivor is when he or she starts clueing in on the behavioral patterns of the toxic person. Victims are no longer caught off guard by the crazy behavior of the harmful individual. When targets can correctly predict the next statement or move by the abuser, the power balance is on its way to being restored. The randomness no longer seems random but calculated and specific with harm as its intent. This is a very important moment in the survivor's ability to deprogram from the onslaught of lies and brainwashing techniques from the psychological abuser.

Fooled was able to see the pattern and it was no longer a surprise. That was the turning point towards recovery and ultimately, freedom.

At first I started to recognize that my mom was a narcissist and from there on I've been reading about the behaviours of these types of people such as trying to sabotage their victim's independence. Also comparing myself to my peers and how they were treated by their parents (helping them succeed in school/work, helping them out emotionally and financially etc) helped me see that I was being sabotaged by my mother and that my dad would stand idly by."

- Nancy

In my book, *Healing from Hidden Abuse: A Journey Through the Stages of Recovery from Psychological Abuse,* I cover Stage Two: Education. This stage occurs early in the recovery roadmap because with education comes healing. Nancy suspected her mom might fit the criteria for Narcissistic Personality Disorder based on observing her mom's chronic behaviors. Nancy then went on to educate herself about how narcissists operate and the common games they play. With this new knowledge, Nancy was prepared to see her mother for who she really was and not what every daughter wishes her mother would be.

Nancy's turning point came when she allowed herself to recognize that she didn't receive the same type of support other people did from their parents. We're often told not to compare our lives to others, and I generally agree. The exception is when we need to recognize that things are not normal in our world. By making honest observations, we can break the chains of denial that can, and will, keep us trapped unless we remove them ourselves.

Actually, I never thought of it as abuse until taking this survey. I've only recently come to understand how he's been abusive in other ways. But he deliberately takes these negative actions. And in the past, when I've panicked or cried because of our financial situations, he's all full of, "Let's pray and trust God," instead of stopping his destructive behavior. I think he likes me being panicked so he can tell me I should stop panicking and trust him/God."

- CJ

In the research project for this book, I asked several questions about the behaviors exhibited by the suspected financial abuser in the participant's life. By asking what lies were told, what threats were made, what basic need they had to go without, what financially criminal behaviors did their abuser engage in and so on, CJ was able to see that in fact, her spouse fit the profile of being exploitive. Sometimes we only need someone to ask us to examine our situation for the answers to come.

CJ brings up a really important point about the moment when her turning point arrived. Instead of changing his harmful ways, CJ's spouse guilted her for not having more faith in him and God. I bet CJ's view of her spouse would have improved if his behavior had permanently changed for the better. This isn't rocket science. People act sleazy yet expect to be trusted without any evidence of their trustworthiness. CJ's reliance on God providing for their needs wasn't the issue, but her husband wanted to deflect responsibility off of himself, so why not throw God into the mix and blame CJ for not having enough faith.

Our CPA let us know he was taking advantage of us."

— Melissa

At times it takes a professional sharing that from their point of view, something is financially off. For Melissa's story, that was within the context of a business arrangement with a toxic individual. In counseling sessions, I frequently find myself sharing that from a mental health perspective, someone is exhibiting traits of being emotionally unsafe for my client. It can be hard and liberating to hear from a trained perspective that yes, they're being abused. Tears from my clients often follow but many will immediately say something such as, "I knew it all along, but I needed someone to confirm it." That confirmation can serve as a turning point.

I just finally realized I was an ATM. I don't know how that finally came through. It just did."

— Melissa

Melissa's mom financially abused her and coming to the realization that your own mother is using you for money is a tough revelation to accept. I know from my own personal experience, a financially exploitive mother can use guilt to cover up their multitude of bad behaviors. They want to hide their exploitive ways so we'll keep blindly helping them, even to our own detriment. The hiding can come in the form of gaslighting. This is when the toxic person tries to get us to doubt our own memory of what was said or not said and what was promised or not promised. When we question our grasp on the truth, the abuser has created the perfect environment to use us without proper boundaries in place.

Melissa came to realize that she was just an ATM to her mom and that became a motivation for change. For myself, I knew for a fact that if I didn't escape my own family dysfunction, I would have suffocated under the weight of carrying the financial burden of my severely exploitive mom.

> *I was completely dependent on him for money while we were married. I was pregnant and 16 when we got married. I had never had a job until I was 30 and wanted to leave. He always said he liked [taking] care of me and who would hire me anyway. I have no experience. It took a few therapy sessions to convince me I could get a job. I got the first one I applied for. It was perfect. I'd get home 30 min after the kids were home from school. This made him feel threatened. He said if I like working so much that I would neglect our kids I can take care of the finances and he will quit his job. I had a part time job making minimum wage and he made $100,000 a year."*

- Jodi

Irrational threats are a form of adult temper tantrums. The pouty suggestion that Jodi could continue working and her husband would quit his job is ridiculous given their difference in income. This is how we know someone was having a man-baby fit. Women abusers do it too. They throw around sarcastic suggestions that no one can take seriously. Why did Jodi's husband become so irritated? Like Jodi said, he was threatened by her working part-time and making minimum wage because it was the first step towards her goal of leaving the abusive marriage. Economic controllers know good and well the power of employment will have on an abuse survivor. That's why they rebel against it.

> *He was arrested on felony charges unrelated to me and then I found out the truth. I found unpaid bill notices, I got notices in the mail, I found papers with my name forged on them, I found IRS notices etc, the electric and water were behind, the house was in foreclosure, the car was about to be repossessed."*

- Michele

Sounds like the truth came crashing down hard all around Michele. That's a lot of information to take in right on the heels of your partner being arrested. His house of cards fell when he was physically removed from keeping his lies spinning.

What are the very first steps you should take if you find out that your family member has been living a secret life of hidden financial fraud? Find yourself one trusted confidant. We all need someone to be authentically transparent with and choosing wisely is critical. If someone starts to question that you must have known something was going on, they can't be your special support person because they will want you to own blame that is not yours. It's very possible that the fraud perpetrated was done so cleanly that the only way to find out was by removing that person from the environment. In Michele's situation, that came with her husband's arrest.

> *Looking back from the outside, I see how he mooched off of me, not even looking for work for more than a year at a time. When I mentioned that I thought he would WANT to work and contribute to the household finances, he flew off the handle, screaming "How much does it really cost you to have me live here?! Why should I have to pay for anything?!" That statement/rage was really the place where my eyes started to open."*

– Kay

Sometimes it's a moment, a sentence, or a certain look by the abuser. Click. Something shifted in that flicker of time and nothing will ever be the same. For Kay, it was hearing that he wasn't going to get a job because Kay would have to pay for herself anyways so what's the problem with him skating by on her life. What most exploitive people don't realize is that being a first-class freeloader is unattractive. Being used for what we can provide kills intimacy for a couple and bonding within a family setting.

One thing that consistently shows up in these types of

relationships is the abuser often tells on themselves. They blurt out all sorts of truth and if we're listening with honesty, we'll learn a lot. Kay got an earful of how her partner viewed his role in her life. From this place of raw honesty, Kay was better situated to make important decisions for her own well-being. For that, I'm grateful he let her know why he hadn't looked for a job in a year. Kay, and all victims of abuse, need to know precisely the level of toxicity they're dealing with in the relationship.

> *Once I lived on my own, I realized how controlling and manipulative he was with my mom and us kids. My mom still lives in constant fear that she will have no money."*
>
> **- Millie**

Watching an innocent parent being mistreated is intensely painful. The feelings of helplessness to change the situation can be overwhelming. Moving out and gaining a fresh perspective allowed Millie to see the depth of dysfunction within her parents' marriage and the household she grew up in. Looking back with educated adult vision is hard but necessary to recover. As Millie heals at a deeper level, she may be able to encourage her mom to find her voice within the marriage or take the necessary steps to gain financial independence. Either way, Millie's journey of healing will be a catalyst for lasting change within her family legacy.

PROTECTION

A critical stage of healing from hidden abuse is starting to protect oneself from continued harm. There's no way to grow and heal without severely limiting or completely stopping the exposure to the maltreatment. In the context of financial abuse and exploitation, the common theme is cutting contact as much as possible from the toxic person. Within the research data for this book, a shockingly high number of participants said that going no contact was the way they protected themselves. Other participants had to remain in some communication because of shared custody of children but they protected themselves by having all of their finances completely out of reach and locked down from the abuser.

> I spoke with a domestic violence hotline after he stole the $6,000 & they advised me to move my remaining money & future paychecks to a new account. It was very difficult to take that step because he had manipulated me into thinking I would then be abusing

him if I cut off his access. I could not
understand why he would do such a
thing & kept thinking it couldn't be real."

- Keleigh

Targets of financial harm are wise to follow the advice the domestic violence advocate gave Keleigh and have their payroll automatically deposited into a separate, solo bank account. Some survivors chose to move that account to a completely different bank from their joint account so no accidental overlaps can occur. Examples of an overlap may be the exploitive individual getting added to the online login system so they can monitor it.

Toxic people often panic when they realize that life is about to change in a big way for them. Keleigh's partner made her feel guilty for protecting her money after he'd already stolen $6,000 from her. Did he really believe she wasn't going to make drastic changes after he illegally financially abused her? It takes quite a large amount of arrogance to believe we can steal from our partner and that she or he will do nothing to stop us from doing it again.

I had to unlearn the financial misinformation (about credit being always bad) my mom fed me. Also, I had to get a credit card in secret. My parents also want me to move back in with them in order to be dependent on them (there's no hope for any real opportunity where they live) and I have to try to make ends meet on my own with only a part-time job. I'm also trying to unlearn the brainwashing from my mother that I will never be able to aim high in my career because I come from a low-income family without the network connections. I'm working on finding a full-time job in my field and earning enough to get my own car so I can break free from my parents trying to get me to be co-dependent on them."

- Nancy

Parental harm is a complex healing process because the poisonous messages from toxic parents become the foundation of our inner voice and personal belief system. When parents are abusive, the social conditioning takes on a dark meaning. Nancy illustrates the exact layer of beliefs that must be re-wired before freedom can be obtained.

If you're a survivor of unhealthy parents, it's helpful to list out as many statements and life rules about finances, your ability to gain independence, and any other limiting core beliefs they taught you. Without properly identifying these parental lies, it's nearly impossible to adequately and completely address them. Instead, these inner beliefs will whisper in the subconscious and hinder growth before you even attempt to change.

We eventually left our church and community because we were not allowed to even present our hearts and our questions regarding tithing to our senior pastors because it was taken as rejecting the authority of the church. Basically, we were told to tithe

*according to membership standards
or step down from our volunteer
positions. So we did just that. And since
then we sit with God and freely have
Him talk to us about our money and
where and to whom He would like us to
give. It's not based on percentages but
needs and mostly God's heart for others.
We also aren't members of any church
but [finding] community in small groups
not connected to church. Because all
churches in our area require tithing and
checking our tithe and membership to
become a part of anything."*

- Babette

Eventually we have to leave oppressive religious or spiritual communities and find freedom with others who view giving and servanthood the same way we do. This applies to those who have been harmed in a Christian church or through another form of religious expression. Financial exploitation isn't limited to just churches. It can come in many faith-based packages, but the signs of abuse are all the same. Money is used as a means of gaining favor with leaders, casting shame on targets, and exploiting their sacred beliefs.

This couple had to walk through the very painful process of being asked to leave a place where they'd worked so hard to fit in and follow the stated rules. When they weren't allowed to come to their leaders with authentic questions, the choices became very limited. Either they would quietly, and without inquiry, accept the demands placed on their wallets or leave the church. Thankfully, Babette and her husband have found community with those who want to serve and give out of the need they see in the world. They're no longer driven by threats of a cursed life for not giving to a certain church and expressing concerns about the health of its leadership.

> *At first, I was thinking divorce is a sin, and would hesitate to file for divorce, but when he refused any counseling or getting treatment for his gambling problems, I had no choice to file for divorce. He was getting [worse] and*

more violent not physically, but verbally and subtle actions. I hide all important documents in a safe place, I got a PO Box address so my mail would not come home. Later, I listened to advice of a good friend to get Id protection and freeze my credit report throughout all credit agencies. I asked the bank for more and faster alerts which I still continue to have, because you never know when he will come up with one of his evil plans."

- Maria

Not all abuse involves physical injury and I'm glad that Maria was able to see that her husband becoming more verbally and covertly abusive was a warning that the environment was growing more unsafe. Psychologically oppressive people and groups never have to physically touch a victim to do tremendous damage that can take years of recovery to move past.

Maria gives us great practical tips to stop the flow of information from reaching the abuser. Since we know they'll use any and every opportunity to gain for themselves, cutting off access is vital for the victim to recover.

> *When my mother ended the relationship I no longer was controlled by her. A few years later, my grandmother passed away and all the grandchildren were given inheritance money but my mother decided I was not worthy of this money. I didn't pursue it, I just let her keep it. Later, when my husband filed for divorce from me, my mother gave him and his new wife the money my grandmother had left to me. I decided to let it go instead of having to deal with her poison. I had the memories of my grandmother and that is worth far more than the money. And my peace of mind not having to fight with my mother is more valuable than the money."*

- Annie

Sometimes we walk away and don't look back. The cruelty of Annie's mother is not uncommon among emotional abusers. Some people actually enjoy making other people feel left out, rejected, and isolated. Annie's mother knew precisely what she was doing by withholding the inheritance and then going so far out of the realm of normal by giving it to Annie's ex and new wife. My goodness. Her mother wasn't even trying to hide her hateful character.

What would have happened if Annie had called her mom upset about either originally not getting the inheritance or later, it going to the ex and new wife? Her mom would have won. This mother took these actions specifically to cause Annie distress and an angry or tearful phone call or visit would have bolstered her mom. A sick game indeed. Her mom may have even let a little smirk cross her face. Have you ever talked to a poisonous person and saw the smirk of enjoyment for the chaos they caused? This is a strong clue that you're dealing with someone who finds entertainment out of harming others.

Setting boundaries. I specifically asked in counseling for account passwords so I could see our finances. I chose to make wise (essentials--food, clothing, etc) purchases without his consent and if he gave me grief, I would remind him he was being controlling. This didn't always work. I also got a part time job and used my money to contribute. His abusive nature wasn't as bad as other people I've seen and I have been able to reach him by setting boundaries and expressing when he's crossed the line."

- Elle

Not all people have to go no contact with a financial exploiter, and Elle shows us key components of how to take back power even while in the relationship. The number one essential ingredient is implementing and maintaining healthy boundaries. They can't be established and then become mushy once the crisis is over. Those who use money to control will return to that baseline if given a chance.

There's a spectrum of toxic people and Elle recognizes that her husband may be on the lower end of the range. We know this to be true because her boundaries and open communication about when he crosses the line are met with changed behaviors. Would Elle's husband have changed on his own without her insisting on counseling for his controlling nature to be addressed? Not likely. Human nature for many people is to keep on doing what works for them, especially if their behaviors go unchallenged.

> *I'm building a business and working a side job. At this point it's still difficult when he misses child support payments, but I'm almost to a point where that won't put me behind on bills when it happens."*
>
> **- Kathy**

Incredible freedom comes from not being dependent on the child support payments to meet household bills. This is especially true when the ex is a financial abuser and has no problem missing payments out of spite or lack of maturity to keep stable employment. How is Kathy getting to the place where she can cover the basics? She's working two jobs. Solid financial protection most frequently comes from the victim taking control over their household budget and income without regard for the support payments. This usually means a season of working and working a lot.

Life is all about making exchanges of time, money, and effort. The energy it takes to scramble when an ex fails, once again, to pay child support on time may be more than the energy it takes to work two or three jobs and know your bills are paid each month. The choice is up to you. From a counseling perspective, I encourage clients to live a life they fully manage and isn't exposed to the whims of a known abuser.

The only way is no contact but I know he will reappear in a few months. That's his MO."

– Rabidpooch

Ah, yes. The good ol' hoover technique. In the world of psychological abuse, hoover or hoovering is when an abuser suddenly reappears after days, months, weeks, or even years to suck the victim back into the toxic dance. Not all abusers hoover but many do. Not all hoovering is pleasant. Sometimes the toxic person will re-emerge by picking a fight, filing a new family court suit, making false accusations – the list of possible ways is endless. On the other hand, some harmful people will hoover through tears of remorse, promises that they've changed, declarations of having found God and are now a completely different person and so on.

The key difference between a person who has really changed is the evidence of sustained improved character choices. I'm not talking about getting publicly re-baptized to show the validity of their new-found faith, but months and years of changed choices that reflect their core nature has gone through a radical transformation. The same principle applies if the now-returned abuser says they see how hurtful they once were but within a short amount of time, they return to vulgar angry outbursts directed at the victim.

Hoovering is a temporary pull back into the relationship

to see if the victim is still hooked. This is an ego boost for toxic people to get an old flame to react emotionally, regardless of whether the emotion is anger or love. Being indifferent is the worst torture for psychological abusers.

> *Filed a list of events with the police, pictures and the evidence of my forged signature on the returned checks."*
>
> **- R**

Documentation serves two purposes. It helps law enforcement and the courts have the proof they need to hopefully protect the victim, and is a wonderful grounding technique for when the doubts creep up on the survivor. The abuser will try and lie his or her way back into the good graces of the victim, and documentation serves as the black and white reality check that can keep them from returning to an unhealthy relationship.

The most effective thing my lawyer did was have our church pastor come in to listen to his testimony about money."

– Nicole

Smart move, counsel. Creating social pressure is an excellent maneuver when dealing with an economically oppressive person. The truth being exposed makes them incredibly uncomfortable and that's a good thing. Lies kept in the dark continue to fester and grow. Another reason Nicole's attorney was wise to invite the pastor was because when the abuser later attempted to shift the story, the truth was already out. Nowhere for the toxic person to maneuver. Checkmate.

> *I began to put a few hundred dollars out of my paycheck into my personal checking account that he did not have access to. I also began storing change and extra money in a hidden place. I also bought gift cards to Walmart, gas cards etc. before I filed for divorce to have money available for buying food etc. after filing."*
>
> **– Angie**

Getting ready to leave a harmful marriage will take quiet preparation. I've been asked by clients if their actions of hiding money and gift cards is the same behavior as the abuser when she or he hid assets. This a great question and the answer is a strong no, they're not the same because the intent is radically different. The intent of the abuser is to oppress, dominate, and create fear. The intent of the victim is to escape. Two complete opposites.

> *I established my own credit, my own bank account, and I left my husband."*
>
> **- Roz**

That pretty much sums up what the majority of participants in the project stated. They took the time to establish themselves financially separate from the abuser and they got out. We all know it's not that simple in real life, but we also don't have to complicate the process more than necessary.

Victims of this form of abuse are smart to make a very short list of what needs to happen to find freedom. This may be very similar to Roz's sentence. How long each of those three things takes isn't the point but rather see it as a brief recap of what has to happen to reach the other side to self-determination.

> *I changed my number, blocked him on social media, cut off contact (mostly) with mutual friends & his family."*
>
> - C

Recovery from harm involves creating a safe space to heal. C did exactly what counselors recommend and that's putting up the necessary walls so the abuser or his/her supporters can't reach her. Why is this level of disconnect necessary? People are playing with fire if they underestimate the ability of a harmful person to weasel their way back into a victim's life. Mutual friends and family frequently don't see the hidden abuse and being exposed to their distorted view of the abuser is damaging to any survivor who's trying to regain autonomy over their life.

"

I am divorcing and I moved across the country into the one bedroom guest house on the farm I grew up on to be away from his manipulation."

- Cake

Sometimes survivors must face big lifestyle changes in order to get the physical separation needed to heal. Is it easy? Not at all, but it's worth every minute of effort. Could Cake's abuser reach out by other means besides showing up at the house since the move? Sure, but that's why blocking phone calls, email, text, social media, and any other form of technology is crucial. Abusive relationships can create a toxic intertwining of two people that must be severed completely or the risk of relapsing back into the poison is too great.

The last few years of the marriage, I removed my name from every joint account except the mortgage. In the end, I filed for divorce. I chose to ignore the repeated counsel of the church that said I must never divorce my wife for anything except adultery. I finally had the courage to stand up for myself and leave the abusive situation."

- Rob

Receiving counsel is important in our lives. It allows us to hear things from a different perspective which expands our thinking on any given topic. Counsel shouldn't be used to be told precisely how to live our lives. We take counsel under consideration and then act accordingly for what's best for our situation. As the person harmed, Rob used his discernment to know that he could no longer stay a target of abuse. He was correct, and I'm sure if we could ask him today if he ever regretted that decision, I have a strong suspicion he'd say absolutely not. Good thing he only took counsel as another opinion and not as absolute truth. Otherwise he might still be trapped in an abusive marriage today.

I say no. Best protection I have."
- Melissa

Indeed. When targets of abuse gain the skills to say no, set limits, and then not fall into the trap of guilt, their whole world shifts. It takes time to work through the conscious and subconscious barriers to become comfortable saying no. There are numerous books on how to stop the patterns of people-pleasing, how to set and maintain healthy boundaries, and why caring for ourselves isn't selfish. If saying no is a challenge, we must invest in the time to unravel the internal lies that we've carried with us probably for years, if not decades.

> *I just cut him out and I no longer make emotional financial decisions. As I said I am also suing him and maintenance enforcement has garnished his wages. I took my car back and gave it to my daughter. That really pissed him off."*
>
> **– Anonymous**

No longer making emotional financial decisions will transform our lives. It's just business and in that mindset, fear has no place to take hold. We learn to remove the pity for the abuser and are better situated to make wise financial choices. For Anonymous, suing for maintenance, having his wages garnished, and taking back the car were non-emotional decisions not out of spite, but a sound business move. The fact that these actions pissed the abuser off was just an added bonus.

> *When he refused to pay his share of our child's private school fees this year, I made sure the Principal of the school and the finance staff were aware of our agreement and sent them copies of our separation agreement. The house I purchased when I left is owned by a family trust and my children are the beneficiaries so no one else can take it from them or me."*
>
> **- Jill**

Survivors in recovery no longer keep the abuser's secrets. They provide the separation agreement to the school and show them exactly who's responsible for payment. That's not being ugly. That is pointing out the truth. Financial abusers and exploiters honestly don't believe their smoke and mirrors life will catch up with them. Jill didn't need to scramble and find a way to make things temporarily easier by paying for the school herself. That wasn't the agreement. She has no need to take on the shame or guilt because her soon-to-be ex failed to follow through on his word.

> "
> *Here are my best tips on where to hide the cash and gift cards: 1. I put some in a box, wrapped it and put a gift tag to my mother. I kept it in my closet. I was confident my husband would never suspect the package contained anything he would be interested in. 2. Among my hanging pants and skirts, I put a pair of (bulky cargo) shorts with the legs sewn shut. The waistband acted as a "pocket" I could quickly drop cash and gift cards into. No one would bother to feel the bottom of a pair of shorts."*
>
> **- Lauri**

Practical ideas for creating an escape plan. Again, not the same as intentionally trying to abuse someone. The leader of a dangerous cult is vastly different than a cult member who's now awake and making a plan to run for freedom. Never let those two truths become blurry.

We have gone no contact with my dad for two years now. We have refused all financial and physical help from any of my family, including my mom and my siblings (not that a lot was offered). We know that the more we allow them to help, the more we'll get sucked back in. It's been very difficult at times, especially with my illness, to not reach out for help. But we have reached out to our church and what little friends we have remaining. Thanks to our church, our kids have a new "grandma" in their lives and I have a new best friend. She takes me to appointments, helps with the kids needs and is always available for hugs. We've had to build up a new family for ourselves."

– Stephanie

Family by choice is my favorite. As a fellow survivor of family abuse, I know how hard it can be to feel like an adult orphan. This is especially painful when our parents are still alive but not safe for contact. The same goes for unhealthy siblings. Stephanie and her immediate family have found the love and support they deserve through surrogate relatives. The beauty of family we choose is that we have the choice to be around healthy adults who hold similar values and can serve as the role models we want for our children.

> *I have to admit I really am not doing much right now but complaining to him. It is too much work, causes too much uproar for the household and never ends up being settled. When the last kid is gone, I will go for my freedom.*"
>
> **- Lucy**

Sometimes we don't know when we will find protection, but we are aware it's desperately needed. That step of honesty is as important as any other tangible actions a victim might take. Lucy, you're not alone in making a plan for when the time is right to execute. Never see that as a position of defeat but rather wisdom and courage.

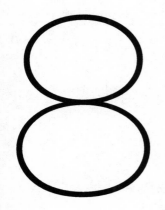

REBUILDING

We have now reached the ever-important point of rebuilding after intense economic harm and often, complete wreckage. I want to say the restoration process from this form of abuse takes longer than most victims expect. There are multiple, compounding layers to the healing transformation that takes place after financial abuse, and moving through those layers is what makes the experience feel like a marathon without a finish line. Learning how other victims rebuilt their lives can serve as a roadmap and hopefully, provide a glimmer of hope.

> *I will finally be finishing my college degree next month after dropping out when our first child was born to stay home. 17 years after I started. I always wanted to finish but he would not allow it."*
>
> **- Rachel**

Going back to school can frequently be part of the rebuilding process. Many victims find that supporting themselves and often children, is impossible without further training to develop a sustainable career path. It may seem like a long journey to head back to school or go through a certificate program. Time is passing anyway, so survivors might as well put the days and months to good use and have lasting financial benefits.

> *I set up many payment plans with the companies he had ran up debts in my name. I ensure I pay these regularly. I have secured a job that will allow me to retrain and gain a better salary in the future. I have set up a small savings account. I have disassociated financial links with him and will continue to do this following the divorce."*
>
> **- hch**

Small steps out of debt is the only option for recovery from financial exploitation. Victims will easily become overwhelmed if they mentally attempt to tackle the entire lump sum. Paralyzing fear can set in and won't help move the situation forward. Making a plan with creditors and celebrating each time the payment is made on time are both perfect, tangible steps. Digging out of debt is a process, not an event. That's why being grateful for each small payment is critical to staying optimistic and forward focused.

> Since I had a big employment gap of 10 years while living with ex narc, I applied for and got a temporary seasonal job of approximately 6 to 8 weeks with a store, hoping to at least close that gap a little, while living with and caring for my elderly mother. They then, after the 6 weeks, kept me on and while it was minimum wage at least I was working. I had to get some public assistance with food stamps to help. My mother then passed away the following year and I then had the rent and utilities to cover myself. I have scrimped and scraped and barely survived it seemed. But I was free. I recently acquired another job and so have been working two jobs, but I have had some

*extra money to buy some needed new
things and I get to decide what and
when! I have been informed that in this
second job they want to promote me.
So I am still working on rebuilding as
it were, I am not there yet, but it is
getting better. Some days I wonder if I
will ever truly rebuild all that was
lost, but I am, in my mind, light years
ahead of where I was while with
the narc."*

- Linda

I love everything about Linda's story because it's real
life. Many targets of abuse have big gaps in their work
history and this can feel like a major roadblock to moving
forward. Linda illustrates exactly how it can be done when
a survivor wants recovery bad enough. I've personally heard
too many excuses for someone not finding work when there
are no real barriers in the way, except perhaps ego. I think
it can come down to how badly someone wants to gain
independence. I'm very aware that there are many issues
that can prevent getting employment, but I'm specifically

addressing those who could but do not. Linda started with a seasonal opportunity and has grown to the point where she's starting to see a little margin in her budget. That's encouraging.

> *Clearing my credit a little at a time and increasing my score.*
>
> *Learning the stock market to invest wisely for retirement*
>
> *Taking classes*
>
> *Reinvesting in a home where I can increase the equity for future sale at retirement."*
>
> **- Laurie**

Most local community colleges offer adult classes on a wide variety of topics, including personal finances. Laurie educated herself in the areas where she had a gap in knowledge and is now able to make more informed decisions for herself. She isn't relying on someone else to tell her how to manage her money but empowered herself to bring wisdom to the table too. Getting professional advice from financial planners, accountants, and others in the related field is fantastic but former targets of abuse must come to those meetings with at least a basic understanding of how it all works. Otherwise, they're setting themselves up to potentially be taken advantage of by an unscrupulous "expert."

> *After opening my own accounts, I had to learn how to handle money. I had never had any so the learning curve was steep and I made mistakes. I purchased my first new car ever a year ago, and qualified for the loan all by myself. I'm still uncertain about my abilities to handle money and feel inadequate to the task. It's part of my recovery in general I guess."*

- CC

Survivors learning to trust their judgement is part of the road to recovery. People will make mistakes and instead of being abused for those honest errors, they learn and keep moving forward. Perfection cannot be the goal. If it is, individuals will find themselves too afraid to try anything new and continue to feel trapped long after the actual abuser is gone.

> *One small step at a time.*
> *That's all I got."*
>
> **- Melissa**

One small step is all that's needed. Perfectly said by Melissa.

> *Hiring a sensitive financial planner,*
> *divorce attorney, estate attorney,*
> *and real estate agent has been helpful*
> *to teach me what is a real budget*
> *and expectation. I had been living*

in a phantom budget household and so many things were hidden or half revealed. I am making sure I ask a lot of professionals a lot of questions. I have also hired an [accountant] that can assess the business / personal tax bills that are owed while still in the divorce process to make sure that a different set of eyes is on that bill. This person is aware of the issues at hand."

– EM

If the financial portfolio is large enough to warrant a team of professionals, survivors of abuse must spend the money upfront. Even though seeing the bank account go down with each payment to another service provider can be scary, survivors will thank themselves in the long run. Not getting wise counsel can definitely have a major impact on an estate of high value. There just is not a way to wing it when so much is at stake.

I don't sniff at any job that comes my way. I go on Facebook and take odd jobs. I've even [shoveled] horse manure. I called all of my creditors and explained that I've been grifted and committed to paying them if they'll just work with me. In 6 years I've paid off $10,000 while keeping a roof over our heads. I still owe $2,000. It's slow going. I've put myself on an austerity program. No TV or house phone. I never go anywhere.

No coffees. I quit the gym. I go to the local food bank. I've sold everything except family heirlooms. I sit here in a dark cold house typing this... keeping the bills down. My nose and fingers are freezing. We only eat meat twice a week. I'm starting a line of clothing to be sold online (I have to buy a computer first) He's not going to win. Success is the revenge. I'm anticipating a lot of revenge."

– Marilyn

Marilyn is a force to be reckoned with! I love her attitude. Her austerity program, as she describes it, may not be for everyone but for Marilyn it seems to bring forth an empowered spirit. No matter what she has to do, Marilyn will not let her abuser win. She's making the necessary sacrifices now that are right for her life and budget. All survivors of financial abuse can implement their own "Marilyn-Plan" in their lives. They may not look the same, but the position of the heart is similar. At the root, it's the willingness to do anything short of things that are illegal, immoral, or unethical to gain financial freedom and stability away from the toxic person.

> *I'm treading water, doing the best I can. I am not rebuilding yet. I'm just maintaining."*
>
> **- Lori**

I want to reframe the idea that rebuilding only involves seeing the bank account balance going up. Maintaining a monthly budget is rebuilding because how many lives were in constant upheaval during the abuse and when money was a weapon? All of them because financial chaos was the norm. Getting to the point where most bills are paid on time, basic needs are met, maybe having a one-off splurge, and putting your head on your pillow at night knowing things are okay for that day is a huge accomplishment post-economic harm. I hope survivors can really grasp the incredible growth that has taken place when they're able to keep their heads above water. That wasn't the case during the abuse.

*1. Budget 2. Simplify 3. Better job
4. Support system 5. Pay off debt
6. Credit Repair 7. Savings."*

- J

We talked earlier about writing down the steps a survivor of abuse would want to see in their journey of healing from financial harm and J has graciously provided one for us. These resonate with the steps I have watched victims of abuse take to climb out from the pit the abuser dug for them.

Let's break these down.

Budget. This will look different for each person because we don't all value the same things. One budget may include more money for eating out because as a single person, that's a form of important socialization and helps to keep them from isolating. Another survivor may need to include vet and grooming bills for their pet that serves as an emotional support companion. Parents will obviously need their budget to reflect the kids' needs and some wants too. There are free basic budgets available online and I'd start with writing down what's being spent right now, not what should be spent. At least get a gauge of where the money is going.

Simplify. Cut out what can be temporarily eliminated. This minimal plan is just for a season of restoration, it's not intended to be a lifelong budget. That would be discouraging for anyone. For now, what can be cut?

Better job. Looking for opportunities to advance in the current position, start a new job, or gain training to become employable are all possible options. The goal is to increase the budget in some way that isn't dependent on the abuser following through with his or her empty promises.

Support system. Some survivors have found support through a community group called Debtors Anonymous. It's helpful for those who want to gain more control over their spending habits and receive support while getting out of debt. A support system might be one friend who's also trying to find stability in their finances and can serve as a sounding board and encouragement.

Pay off debts. It's important to contact debtors and arrange for re-payment if they're willing. Survivors should be prepared that the person on the other end may not like their job or is having a bad day and could have an attitude. We have to remember it isn't personal. Set up the plans that can be arranged and remember to celebrate every time that payment clears. It's one more step to freedom.

Credit repair. There are services that will monitor credit for new applications and provide an alert. Many participants of the study specifically said they use LifeLock. That's not an endorsement, but it was the number one credit protection service that was mentioned several times by former targets of financial abuse. Many survivors also put alerts on their bank accounts to ding them with each purchase. If something odd pops up, they can take immediate action to quickly stop any financial hemorrhaging that would occur from fraud against their account.

One very helpful way to rebuild credit is with the use of a secure credit card. This is where the individual puts a down payment in the sum similar to $300 or $500 and the credit card has a credit limit matching the down payment. The individual then uses the card like a normal credit card and pays off what's charged each month, not touching the down payment to pay the bill. This is a very helpful mechanism to rebuild a damaged credit score.

Savings. One of the most effective ways to start saving is to open a free online account with one of the larger investment companies. It doesn't take long to get a brokerage account started and there are useful educational tools on their websites to help guide a new investor. Once the account is open, link it to personal banking and have a set amount taken out each month. It doesn't matter if that amount is $10. Start somewhere. There's power in being intentional about a certain goal. The survivor will no longer need to start saving, but start saving more. There's a huge difference between the two.

I am on my own.
I am my own responsibility."

– Aimee

I specifically chose this quote from Aimee to complete the stories from targets, victims, and survivors of financial abuse. I did so because Aimee has captured the heart of the recovery process. Being comfortable with independence, not rescuing an abuser, setting needed limits with people, and looking towards the future with hope is the foundation of healing from hidden abuse.

Thank you for joining me on this journey of learning more about the secret world of financial abuse and exploitation that is happening all around us. If you are a survivor of this form of harm, I hope your experiences have been represented here in a way that is honoring to what you have lived through. It is my greatest desire that others will pick up where I have left off on this topic and help to make lasting changes in our family courts, criminal laws, and expand our collective knowledge about abuse that comes in the form of economic destruction. It is time for all manifestations of psychological abuse to come out from the shadows and stand in full view so that victims are no longer left isolated and without adequate resources to find help, recovery, and ultimately, restoration.